THE WONDERS OF GOD

THE WONDERS OF GOD

WILLIAM MACDONALD

GOSPEL FOLIO PRESS
P. O. Box 2041, Grand Rapids MI 49501-2041
Available in the UK from
JOHN RITCHIE LTD., Kilmarnock, Scotland

THE WONDERS OF GOD
by William MacDonald

Published by Gospel Folio Press
P. O. Box 2041
Grand Rapids, MI 49501-2041

ISBN 1-882701-25-9

Cover design by J. B. Nicholson, Jr.

Printed in the United States of America

CONTENTS

PART I

The Wonders of God in Creation

O Lord, how manifold are Your works!
In wisdom You have made them all.
Psalm 104:24

THE WONDERS OF GOD IN CREATION

I will praise You, O Lord, with my whole heart;
I will tell of all Your marvelous works (Ps. 9:1).

The works of the Lord are great,
Studied by all who have pleasure in them (Ps. 111:2).

All Your works shall praise You, O Lord,
And all Your saints shall bless You (Ps. 145:10).

The whole earth is full of His glory (Isa. 6:3).

The works of the Lord are wonderful beyond description. Everything that He has created is a marvel. A single cell is as amazing in its order and complexity as the starry heavens. The great English preacher Charles Haddon Spurgeon said it well:

> In design, in size, in number, in excellence, all the works of the Lord are great. In some point of view or other each one of the productions of His power, or the deeds of His wisdom, will appear to be great to the wise in heart. Those who love their Maker delight in His handiworks, they perceive that there is more in them than appears on the surface, and therefore they bend their minds to study and understand them. The devout naturalist ransacks nature...and hoards up each grain of its golden truth.[1]

THE WONDER OF THE HUMAN BODY

Who has made man's mouth? Or who makes the mute, the deaf, the seeing, or the blind? Have not I, the Lord? (Ex. 4:11).

I will praise You, for I am fearfully and wonderfully made.
Marvelous are Your works,
And that my soul knows very well (Ps. 139:14).

The blueprint for the human body is contained in the DNA molecule. It is incredible that anything so minuscule could contain so much! If all the DNA in the body could be somehow unwound and the segments spliced together, the resulting thread would reach to the sun and back four hundred times! Yet all the body's genes (where the DNA is found) would fit into a block no bigger than an ice cube. The information stored in the human DNA would fill an average home library of 100 volumes.

The body is a marvel of diversity and unity. Although it has billions of parts, they all work together, enabling a person to eat, drink, walk, run, jump, see, hear, touch, taste, smell, learn, think, and remember.

The brain is the general headquarters of this complex masterpiece. Orders go out from it and, when obeyed, generally maintain a healthy, functioning body.

Billions of people have lived and are living, yet *no two are exactly alike*. Fortunately for honest people, criminals run up against this inescapable fact when their fingerprints match those at the scene of the crime. Now we have what is known as *genetic fingerprinting*, where chemical sequences of DNA found in a person's blood, sweat, or saliva are analyzed. What are the chances that two parents will produce identical children? The innumerable possible combinations of DNA renders the likelihood so remote as to be unworthy of consideration. Someone has estimated the odds as 70 trillion to one—which is another way of saying infinitesimal.

Think of the extraordinary coordination of mind, bones, and muscles that enables people to perform such extraordinary feats of skill, strength, speed, and endurance as lifting 6,270 pounds of dead weight; running for 26 miles in a marathon; running over 27 miles per hour; performing a high jump of 8 feet; and climbing over 29,000 feet to the top of Mount Everest.

Of course, the body needs food to provide this energy. As the food is chewed, it mixes with saliva, which lubricates it and often begins the breakdown of starches. It is propelled through the esophagus to the stomach, whose assignment is to break it down further with just the right amount of acid. (Otherwise the person enjoying the gourmet meal might have to rush off to the hospital with an ulcer!) The next stop is the small intestine which deftly transfers vitamins, minerals, and nutrients to the blood stream. The large intestine absorbs the liquids. All this takes place without any conscious prompting or action on the part of the eater.

When we enjoy a meal of filet mignon steak, baked potatoes loaded with butter and bacon bits, mixed vegetables, and salad, we are carelessly unaware of the marvelous processes that are taking place in our body. The food is assimilated in such a way that some is assigned to bone, some to flesh, blood, muscles, nerves, other to hair, teeth or eyes. And not only is every part of the body nourished and renewed, but also some of the food becomes energy that enables us to get up from the table when the last forkful of pie à la mode is consumed. How does the food know what part it is supposed to play?

Sight

Sight is the extraordinary faculty by which light is translated into information which reveals the colors and shapes of our environment. In the simple act of looking, you are unaware of the billions of calculations that are going on as the brain teams up with the eyes to show you the words you are now reading.

The human eye is a combination of still camera, movie camera, and light meter. It has automatic focusing, wide-angle lens, zoom lens, and full-color instantaneous reproduction.

The brain has been called an enchanted loom that takes the electrical signals from rods and cones in the eyes and weaves those bits of information into a tapestry portrait of what is in front of you.[2]

Our eyes enable us to distinguish distances, a must for all drivers of vehicles who don't want to hit someone else! They provide depth perception, which is imperative for the pilot as he eases the plane down onto the runway. They seem to be quite simple members of the body, yet they contain six million cones that serve as receptors and millions of things called rods. These rods contains millions of molecules of rhodopsin, a photosensitive pigment which is especially important for vision in dim light.

The human eye sees things as upside-down images, but the brain comes to our rescue in such a way that we see them as they should be—rightside up.

If you gaze at an object, then look away so that it is no longer visible, you can reach out your hand and touch the object. Sight teams up with memory to make this possible, yet scientists do not fully understand this simple ability.

A complete explanation of the marvel of human eyesight eludes scientists. It has been aptly called "the holy grail of vision research."

Hearing

It is nothing short of astounding how the inner ear receives words in the form of sound waves, converts them to nerve impulses, and transmits those impulses to the brain. The auditory cortex processes the information and sends it on to the brain's left hemisphere, which is the language department. Yet people seldom appreciate their hearing until they lose it.

Think of the marvelous filtering mechanism that allows a mother to sleep through her husband's raucous snoring, yet awakens her in a flash when she hears her baby cry in another room! One night a new father awoke to answer the phone. Getting out of bed, he tripped on a toy and crashed to the floor. His wife slept soundly. As he lay there, there was a slight cough from the baby's room. The mother awoke instantly and raced to the baby. On returning, she saw her husband on the floor and asked, "What on earth are you doing down there?"

Ears are also essential for maintaining equilibrium. When the inner ear is out of sorts, the world around us spins dizzily. They call it *vertigo*.

Speech

Talking comes almost as naturally to us as breathing. But how do we do it? You can live a normal life without knowing the mechanics of speech, but here they are: When we want to say something, our brain sends a signal to the lungs to expel air. The air rushes up the throat to the larynx and in the process vibrates the vocal chords. If we want our words to be high-pitched, our brain tells certain muscles to tighten the chords. When the chords are relaxed, the pitch is lower. Of course, the lips, tongue, and jaw cooperate in the process to produce intelligible speech or pleasurable song (hopefully).

Touch

Did you ever think how amazing your skin is? It does not allow water to penetrate *inwardly*, but does allow it to *exit*. It enables you to know whether you are holding one sheet of paper or two. It measures pressure and discerns heat and cold. Shaking hands, kissing—the stimulation of our sense of touch is essential to a normal life.

The largest "organ" of the body is the skin, a birthday suit that clothes us through all of life. It weighs, on the average, six pounds, and covers two square yards, give or take a little. We can be thankful that it has tremendous elasticity, and that its million and more nerve endings enable us to distinguish a host of sensations.

Smell

It is estimated that the average person can identify at least 4,000 odors. A few people have the capacity to discern 10,000! But that's nothing to brag about! A dog can surpass a human being in this skill. A third of its brain is devoted to scent. That's why certain dogs are used to find lost persons and track down criminals. They have extraordinary power to sense scents. The nose knows fragrances that are indistinguishable in laboratory experiments.

It is truly amazing that we can recognize an odor we may not have smelled since childhood. How can a distinctive odor be stored that long in the brain? Some scents trigger a flow of saliva, others bring forth the single word: *"Yuk!"*

The Hand

Nothing is as handy as the hand. If you make a list of all the tasks that a human hand has to perform and then feed that list into a computer—and if the computer has the software that will make a graphic design of a tool that would best accomplish all those tasks—the computer would show a perfect reproduction of a human hand.

The hand is so important that a special area of the brain is assigned to it, quite distinct from the area associated with the fingers.

The Brain

Who has put wisdom in the mind,
Or who has given understanding to the heart? (Job 38:36)

The average adult brain, weighing about three pounds, enables its owner to learn (animals can do that) and to think or reason (animals can't do that). It can understand, memorize, and retrieve information.

All the experiences we have ever had and all the knowledge we have acquired are stored in the mind. What a tremendous file! It is true that we can't always remember it all, but it's all there, waiting to be recalled.

A brain surgeon, using a local anesthetic on a patient, can touch various parts of the brain with an electrode and revive the past:

"What is it now?"

"I am in the hospital, giving birth to my first child. I can smell something like ether."

"And what is it now?"

"Our whole family is in the living room of our home, listening to *Aïda*."

Just think of all the knowledge and experiences that are stashed away in your brain!

Of all the marvels of the human body, none is more mind-boggling than the brain. We decide to think about our summer vacation, for instance, and presto! the process begins. But how does it begin? In our thirst we lift a glass of ice water to our lips. But how did the brain activate the hand to lift the glass? Scientists say that our thoughts and intentions are created by a combination of electrical currents and chemicals. But how are they turned on? The fact is that we know very little about the operation of the brain, and there is little hope that we will ever be able to fathom it fully. The interaction of the brain and the body presents biology with its ultimate challenge.

Even scientists who are not Christians stand in awe of the human brain, though frequently they stubbornly refuse to acknowledge its Designer. It is so complex that no computer will ever be able to match it.

Edmund Bolles called it "the most complicated structure in the known universe."[3]

Dr. Michael Denton, in *Evolution: A Theory in Crisis*, concludes that "it would take an eternity" for engineers to assemble an object even remotely resembling the human brain, using the most sophisticated engineering techniques.[4]

Oxford Professor Roger Penrose, evolutionist and author of the 1989 book, *The Emperor's New Mind*, cautions against stating that the human brain is just a complex computer or that a computer will ever be able to think (i.e., artificial intelligence): "The very fact that the mind leads us to truths that are not computable convinces me that a computer can never duplicate the mind."[5]

The brain's sophistication has also prompted prolific science writer (and evolutionist) Isaac Asimov to acknowledge that "in Man is a three-pound brain which, as far as we know, is the most complex and orderly arrangement of matter in the universe."[6]

The information that can be held in the human brain is staggering in its extent. It has been estimated that it would fill some twenty million volumes. Many of the world's largest libraries do not have more than that.

Christians have been in the forefront of those who acknowledge the order and complexity of the brain. Drs. DeYoung and Bliss write:

> Our brain [is] the greatest concentration of chemo-neurological order and complexity in the physical universe. It is a video camera and library, a computer and communication system, all in one. And the more the brain is used, the better it becomes! A detailed picture of the human brain is slowly emerging, the origin of which seems entirely beyond comprehension from a naturalistic point of view. We see remark-

> able purpose and interdependence within the brain—every part works for the benefit of the whole. Such features are not totally understood; the brain is unable fully to understand itself. As always, we cannot fully understand the created, intricate details of the present-day world.[7]

Jerry Bergman writes:

One scientist estimated that our brain, on the average, processes over 10,000 thoughts and concepts each day—and some people process a much greater number.[8]

Memory

American biblical scholar Robert Dick Wilson learned 45 ancient languages and dialects. A group of Jewish memory experts memorized the 12 large volumes of the Babylonian Talmud.

Arturo Toscanini was reputedly able to study a symphony score and file it away in his memory, perfect to the last note.

In Rome, Wolfgang Amadeus Mozart heard the Sistine Choir in the famous *Miserere* by Gregorio Allegri. This music was considered the private possession of the choir, and was not available for public distribution. After listening to it, Mozart copied it out *from memory.*

In 1858, Paul Morphy played eight games of chess simultaneously *while blindfolded!* His opponents were eight of the best players in Paris. As they called out their moves, he remembered the positions and dictated the replies. Anyone who can play one game without seeing the board is remarkable. Here was a person who played eight at once. No wonder he was called the Mozart of chess![9]

Heredity

We all know how children often resemble their parents in facial appearance, in color and texture of hair, in bone structure, and even in gait. But how is it possible that a person can inherit poetic ability? How can the genes transmit *skill* as an artist or a musician? Yet they do!

Emotions—Fear, Anger, Sorrow, Depression

In times of crisis, the body automatically pumps adrenaline

into the system as it is needed. How does the body know?

The Circulatory System

The heart begins beating four weeks after a baby's conception and continues faithfully for an entire lifetime. It pumps 100,000 times a day, sometimes for over 100 years—without stopping for maintenance or repairs.

No bigger than a fist, this tireless wonder pumps five quarts of blood a minute, distributing oxygen, carrying away waste, and regulating the body's temperature. In a 70-year lifetime, it beats 2.3 billion times without external lubrication. What a marvel!

The Wonders of Reproduction

Conception and the miracle of birth are extraordinary. We start off as a fertilized egg about the size of the dot over the letter i. Yet in that dot is programmed everything that our body will ever be—the shape of the chin, the color of the eyes and hair, our height, sex, brain capacity, voice, and general appearance. Everything! As the fertilized egg develops, cells assume different forms—flesh, bones, muscles, nerves and tendons—all the parts of the body. In a way that baffles science, some cells seem to know that they are supposed to form kidneys. So they move to where the kidneys ought to be and start multiplying. Others cleverly form the lungs in exactly the right place. And if this is not amazing enough, they seem to know the proper timing. For instance, veins must be in place in time to support organs that depend on them. This wonderful process of multiplication, positioning, and timing produces a beating heart in four weeks, a developing brain in three months. The baby makes his or her debut in nine months. But if, for some reason, a glitch takes place in the process, the mother's body seems to know that there would be a malformation and so rejects the fetus. How does it know?

Scientists acknowledge that the appearance of a living fetus in the womb is still a mystery. How is life produced? Textbooks on biology can detail the sequence of events that lead to conception, gestation, and birth. They explain *what* happens but the mystery of *how* and *why* remains.

Relation Between the Mental and the Physical

Medical science knows today that there is a close link between the *mental* and *physical*. We know, in addition, that there is a close link between the *spiritual* and *physical*. Worry causes ulcers. People who are aggressive, achievement-oriented, and impatient are more prone to heart attacks than those who are more relaxed. Tension can cause any number of ailments. Sin often brings on sickness and death. Psychosomatic medicine is the field that studies these relationships.

The Body's Healing Power

Why did the doctor tell you to take two aspirins and call him in the morning? Because he knows that most things are *better* by the morning! The body has mechanisms to fight fever, viruses, and infections, and they do it very efficiently.

The immune system of the body is a mechanism *par excellence*. The efficient and sophisticated defenses of the human system against disease are nothing short of a marvel. As soon as a germ or virus invades, the system literally swings into action to repel the intruder. Cells, blood, and organs mobilize instantly without any conscious effort on the part of the person. They attack the harmful bacteria, either destroying it or halting its progress. In some cases, the person is henceforth permanently immunized against that particular disease.

Think of how the body sends out warning signals when all is not well—fever, inflammation, pain, and bleeding, for example. But these are not only red flags—they are also part of the body's way of actually *combatting* the trouble.

And think how the body knows the difference between one of its own organs and one that is transplanted. How does it know what to accept and what to reject?

The Spirit and Soul

Man is a tripartite being, composed of *spirit*, *soul*, and *body* (1 Thess. 5:23). The body is the structure in which the spirit and soul dwell. When they leave, the body is dead. The spirit enables a person to have fellowship with God. The soul enables him to interact with his environment, and is the seat of his emotions.

The Bible clearly teaches that there is spiritual intelligence quite apart from the brain. Disembodied spirits in heaven and in Hades (Acts 2) have knowledge, memory, speech, and emotions.

No one can deny that there is a marvelous design in creation. If there is *design*, how can anyone deny that there is a *Designer?*

THE STARRY HEAVENS

When I consider Your heavens,
The work of Your fingers,
The moon and the stars, which You have ordained,
What is man that You are mindful of him,
And the son of man that You visit Him (Ps.8:3-4).

The heavens declare the glory of God;
And the firmament shows His handiwork.
Day unto day utters speech,
And night unto night reveals knowledge.
There is no speech nor language
Where their voice is not heard (Ps. 19:1-3).

He counts the number of the stars;
He calls them all by name.
Great is our Lord, and mighty in power;
His understanding is infinite (Ps. 147:4-5).

He made the Pleiades and Orion;...
The Lord is His name (Amos 5:8).

Before thinking about the stars in the heavens, we might well ask ourselves, "Who made the universe that contains all the heavenly bodies? In other words, who made space?" The thought boggles the mind, as well it might.

Spurgeon said that "any part of the creation has more instruction in it than the human mind will ever exhaust, but the celestial realm is peculiarly rich in spiritual lore."[10]

If it cost a penny to travel a thousand miles, a cruise to the moon would be only $2.38. But if you wanted to go to the sun, the one-way ticket would cost $930. And a trip to the nearest star would be—hold onto your hat—$260 million.

With the naked eye, we can see about 5,000 stars. With a homestyle telescope, 2,000,000 come into view. The Hubble telescope enlarges our vision to billions and billions. Sir James Jeans said that there are probably as many stars as there are grains of sand on all the beaches of the world. Yet the stars are not crowded together. Rather, they are like lonely lightships on an ocean without shores.

Astronomers can see objects 10 billion light years away. A light year is the distance light travels in a year. Since it travels 186,282 miles a second, light covers six trillion miles a year.

When we look into the heavens at night, we are seeing history, not current events. For example, we see the star Rigel where it was 540 years ago. It has taken that long for its light to reach our planet.

The galaxies seem to be traveling away from us at enormous speeds. If some are traveling at the speed of light—too bad!—we will never see them.

As far as size is concerned, our planet is very insignificant in the universe. It is like a speck of cosmic dust. A thousand earths could fit inside Jupiter. It would take 1,300,000 earths to equal the size of one sun.

The Milky Way contains 300 million suns. Some stars could hold 500 million suns the size of ours.

It is estimated that there are some 100 billion galaxies and 100 billion stars in every galaxy. Einstein believed that we have scanned with our largest telescopes only a billionth of "theoretical space." If we were somehow projected out into the cosmos, the chance that we would land on any heavenly body is infinitesimally small—not worth mentioning. The stars are, on the average, light years apart.

Even unbelieving scientists are forced to admit that the galaxies reveal a universal and extraordinary order and beauty. An astronomer said that galaxies are to astronomy what atoms are to physics. Another astronomer spoke of the awe which the universe inspires because of the intricate and subtle way it is put together.

Actually the size of the universe is beyond human comprehension. It is profuse with amazing facts, with astounding interrelationships, and with awesome mechanical precision.

Wonder of wonders! Vast surprise!
Can bigger wonder be?—
That He who built the starry skies
Once bled and died for me.
—Author unknown

A recent scientific article reported that the universe is so finely tuned that the odds of achieving it by chance would be the same as throwing an imaginary microscopic dart across the universe to the most distant quasar and hitting a bull's eye one millimeter in diameter. Actually this graphic illustration is pathetically inadequate. The odds are infinitely *less* than that!

Planet Earth

...what may be known of God is manifest in them [people], for God has showed it to them. For since the creation of the world His invisible attributes are clearly seen, being understood by the things that are made, even His eternal power and Godhead, so that they are without excuse (Rom. 1:19-20).

When God finished the work of creation, He saw that "it was very good." Not one of us can ever realize how "very good" it *was!* Everything the Lord does is perfect.

This is never more true than of the planet on which we live. The Creator designed the earth so that it would be absolutely ideal for human habitation, as to beauty, comfort, and economy. As far as we know, no other planet in the universe can boast the advantages of ours.

For instance, it is just the right distance from the sun—93 million miles. If it were more or less, life could not survive.

The earth itself is just the right size. If it were different, its blanket of atmosphere would be too dense or too thin, and all life would become extinct.

The tilt of the earth is what causes the four seasons, and makes the cultivation of the land possible. Without it, most of the surface of the earth would be a vast Sahara.

The earth's rotation is not accidental. Finely tuned to just the right speed in its orbit around the sun, it disburses the warmth of the sun uniformly and generates winds and ocean currents.

The atmosphere is just what we humans need as to its composition and density. Oxygen makes up 21% and nitrogen 78% of the air we breathe. Every one of us is living proof of its suitability. Take a deep breath and praise the Lord!

God designed the ozone layer to protect us from the harmful ultraviolet rays of the sun. Now man is poking holes in the ozone with his uncontrolled chemical emissions, but this is his problem, not the Lord's.

Water is indispensable. So our generous God covered four-fifths of the earth's surface with it in streams, lakes, and seas. Science knows of no other planet that has a permanent supply of water in liquid form. It is a major constituent of all living matter. It is good as a solvent for the laundry, as a coolant for beverages, and as steam for power plants.

Unlike most compounds, water is less dense as a solid than as a liquid (ice floats in water). As a result, when a lake freezes in the winter, it does so from the top down. Eventually the layers of ice insulate the remainder of the water from the cold winter air, and at certain depths the freezing process stops. If, as with most compounds, water was denser as a solid than as a liquid, lakes would freeze from the bottom up, and all the fish would be frozen solid.

To think that all this happened by chance is unrealistic. Says Stuart Nevins, "It is akin to supposing that the Mona Lisa came into existence from globs of paint being hurled at a canvas."[11]

WONDERS ON THE LAND

Wild animals and all cattle,
Small creatures and flying birds…
Let them praise the name of the Lord (Ps. 148:10, 13).

The Lion

The "king of the beasts" actively participates in bringing up his young. Together with the lioness, he watches over the cubs, feeds them, and joins in their games. He is the only member of the cat family that manifests the paternal instinct.

The Giraffe

The baby giraffe is handed over to a collective "nursery,"

which is watched over tenderly by the entire herd, though each of the young is the special responsibility of one particular "nursemaid."[12]

The Chamois

Chamois live in herds of 20, 30, sometimes even 100. Each herd is led by one experienced *female*.

The Gecko

The gecko's adhesive fingers are unique in the animal kingdom, and it is only recently that their secret has been discovered. Their webbed fingers have thin sheets of skin of all shapes and dimensions on their undersides that can stretch in any direction. These are covered with several million very tiny bumps that solidly grip the most difficult surfaces. In addition, the skin is wrinkled and stretches and folds back, thus creating a vacuum between the animal's paws and the supporting surface.[13]

The Roe Deer

As fertilization of the roe deer occurs in July or August, the young should logically be born in the winter, when they would be endangered by hunger, the cold, and the more than usually hungry carnivores of the forest. But the fawn is cleverly protected by Divine wisdom. The implantation of the fertilized ovum in the wall of the uterus is postponed, and the embryo only begins to develop in December. Thus the fawn is born in May, nine months after conception, when the leaves can provide shelter and its enemies are less hungry.[14]

The Platypus

The unique duck-billed platypus is poisonous like a snake, lays eggs like a bird, and swims like a beaver.

The Domestic Cat

It is not only wild or unusual animals, such as the lion and the platypus, that have wonderful built-in characteristics. As an old folk song puts it, "We thought he was a gonner, but the cat came back."

One cat came home after being gone for eight years:

A homeowner in Bancroft, Wisconsin, said he heard a cat meowing on the front porch. When he opened the door, a big, long-haired, gray male cat walked in, checked things out, began purring, and then jumped up on his favorite chair. Family members couldn't believe their eyes. But when they compared the cat to pictures taken eight years earlier, they could only conclude that Clem the cat had come home.[15]

WONDERS IN THE SEA

The Blue Whale

Here is a description of the earth's largest creature:

> [It is] longer than three dump trucks, heavier than 110 Honda Civics, and has a heart the size of a Volkswagen Beetle. How much food does it take to sustain such an animal? Try 4 tons of krill a day—that's 3 million calories! Even a baby blue whale can put away 100 gallons of milk every 24 hours. When a blue whale surfaces, it takes in the largest breath of air of any living thing on the planet. Its spray shoots higher into the air than the height of a telephone pole.[16]

The Dolphin

The female dolphins of a herd surround a pregnant dolphin, warding off all dangers while the mother swims slowly and gives birth to her calf.

The Sea Horse

Unique in the animal kingdom, the male sea horse becomes "pregnant." Several females lay their eggs in his brooding pouch, which swells as the larvae develop. After a gestation period of 6 to 8 weeks, the young are expelled into the water.[17]

WONDERS IN THE AIR

Some of God's most widely watched and admired creatures are airborne. For sheer variety, color, number, and song, birds can hardly be matched.

And in the insect world there are the multicolored and delicate butterflies. Who has not chased such a brilliant-winged charmer as a child on a sunny day?

Even more remarkable are the scientific facts about many of these little flying wonders.

The Migratory Instinct

The migration of birds is enough to stagger the imagination. The birds know their proper destination—the right place for them to nest, feed, and winter. One type of sandpiper travels 9,900 miles to get to its winter home.

The Arctic tern makes two trips a year from one pole to the other—11,000 miles without compass or maps.

Migratory birds have a built-in navigational system. It would be fatal for them to drift off course, so they constantly adjust for adverse winds. Men have repeatedly tried to disorient them by clever experiments but always in vain.

The Lesser Whitethroat Warbler

Warbling may not be the main achievement of this little feathered friend. Its migratory instinct is astounding. After summering in Germany, it heads south for a warmer climate. In doing so, however, it seems to be guilty of parental neglect, because it leaves its little ones behind.

Weeks later the young warblers take off and fly over thousands of miles of unfamiliar and uncharted landscape to catch up with the parent birds. Apparently they have a built in navigational system that takes account of longitude, latitude, and the stellar heavens. With unsurpassed accuracy, they arrive at the right place at the right time.[18]

The Sea Gull

When we think of the wonders of the universe, we are not apt to think of the ubiquitous sea gull. One of God's scavengers, this bird seems to be in every place where there is water and in many places where there is not.

Those who have traveled across an ocean have seen sea gulls following the ship, looking for an occasional handout. There they are—in the middle of the ocean, far removed from land or fresh water.

Which raises an interesting question. What do sea gulls drink when they are thousands of miles from land? Dismiss the idea of seawater right away. If they drank salt water, they would have a very short life expectancy. Yet they must have water.

The answer is quite unusual. They imbibe saltwater because that is all that is available. The saltwater passes through a filter membrane, a marvelous desalinization mechanism. The salt is separated and emerges as a teardrop from the gull's eye. The fresh water goes down into the gullet where it is needed.

So simple, and yet man cannot duplicate it inexpensively!

Clam Chowder

When I was a boy, we used to visit friends at Brewster Beach, Massachusetts. There the tide goes out a mile. We would walk out after the retreating waves and dig for sea clams, king-sized members of the bivalve mollusk family.

Often we would be spellbound as we watched the sea gulls. They knew when a clam was near the surface of the sand. High up they could probably see the tiny geyser that betrayed the presence of the clam. They would swoop like a dive-bomber and with great precision fix their bills on the luckless bivalve, then rise up in a graceful arc.

Only one problem. The clam was well packaged. How could the sea gull get at the succulent meat that was encased between two powerful shells? No problem. After reaching a height that was somehow guaranteed to be correct, the canny bird would drop the clam, fold its wings, and follow down with the force of gravity. The clam would hit the sand and break open. The sea gull would spread its wings and without coming to a stop would pick up the meat and fly away to enjoy a New England clam dinner.

Who Taught the Bird?

A hunter in South America was attracted by the cries of a distressed bird. A venomous snake was crawling up the tree toward the nest. The bird flew away for a short time, then returned with a leaf-covered twig and laid it across the top of the nest. "The snake twisted round and up the tree; then glided along the branch to the nest. He poised himself to strike; then suddenly throwing his head back as if he had received a deadly blow, he recoiled and writhed away down the tree as fast as possible." Later the hunter learned that the leaf was from a bush that is deadly poison to snakes. The sight and smell of the leaf caused the snake to retreat.[19]

Have you ever seen a bird playing the broken wing act? When a cat crouches and creeps toward a tree that houses a nest with little birds, the mother can waste no time in protecting her young. She descends to a foot or two off the ground, then flies away from the tree, bouncing up and down off the ground as if one wing was broken. No self-respecting cat can resist chasing her. But in the process the feline is drawn away from the tree and distracted by the prospect of feasting on a seemingly disabled bird. Guess who wins!

The Hummingbird

It can hover, power-dive, fly forward or backward, up, down, or sideways, and even upside down to escape predators. But it can't float with wings held still. It has the most rapid wing beats of any bird. Its heart beats 1,260 times a minute. All hummingbirds weigh less than an ounce, some only two grams. Its brain, though tiny, is the largest proportionately of any bird.

In migration some hummingbirds fly 500 miles nonstop over the Gulf of Mexico. They average 25 miles per hour for 20 hours on a gram of stored fat. This is tremendous fuel efficiency!

The Weaver Bird

These master builders construct their nests with incredible skill. They lace, weave, and knot varied materials together tightly, anchor their masterpieces in the branches of trees with knotted cables, and then connect them by hanging bridges.

The Titmouse

This bird is more threatened by starvation than by the cold; if it is without food for 24 hours it dies. Our Lord says that the heavenly Father will feed the birds of the air (Matthew 6:26), and the titmouse lives according to this promise, happy and completely unconcerned about tomorrow. It is all delicate grace and airy lightness.

The Sand Grouse

The sand grouse broods her young on the Namib Desert where the temperature sometimes reaches 170 degrees Fahrenheit. She cools herself in the sweltering heat by fluttering her throat, thus creating a rapid exchange of air. Even more remarkable is the way the male grouse provides water for the chicks every day. Each morning he flies to a distant water hole to drink. Because many enemies gather at the water, most of these birds can stay only a few seconds. But the male parent stays longer in order to immerse its breast feathers in the water. These feathers are cleverly designed to hold water that can be carried back to the young. He flies back to the young—often as much as 50 miles—heavily laden with water. As soon as he reaches the chicks, they instinctively know where to drink.[20]

The Red-cockaded Woodpecker

In the pine forests of Georgia and Florida, the red-cockaded woodpecker drills its hole for a nest in a living pine, not one that has been incinerated by lightning. It chooses a place low down on the trunk. The wood is so hard that it sometimes takes several of these birds two years to complete the task. In the process, yellow resinous sap seeps out of the hole where the outer layers have been breached. The woodpecker diverts the flow of resin into pits it drills below and above the hole. This yellow resin makes the hole where the bird raises its young very conspicuously.

Enter, "stage left," the rat snake, a good climber, adept at robbing nests of their young. Since the hole is low on the trunk, it is easily accessible to the snake. But—and here's the big but—the chemicals in the resin are extremely abhorrent to the snake. When it draws near, it arches its body, drops to the ground, and slithers away.[21]

The Monarch Butterfly

Don't judge this butterfly by its size! After wintering in fir trees on a plateau in central Mexico, monarch butterflies start their annual flight to northern latitudes for a more congenial summer. Along the way they pause long enough to lay eggs on milkweed and thus insure the perpetuation of their species.

Then an amazing thing happens. As winter approaches, the new generation flies to the plateau in central Mexico where they have never been before. Who directs them? Since birth they have had no contact with the old monarchs, no coaching as to the route to take. Yet they go to the ancestral home with unerring skill.

The Ant

An ant lives 15 to 20 years. It is blind or nearly blind, but is guided by smell, taste, and touch. It is able to carry more than 50 times its own weight. This is the equivalent of a man lifting 3 automobiles at the same time!

The Ichneumon Wasp

These wasps inject their ovipositor in the coat of fat around a larva. Neither the best hidden caterpillar nor the smallest louse escapes it. No suitable host is spared; even a chrysalis will do. Ichneumon wasps with long ovipositors seek out larvae buried in the trunks of trees. They drill into the wood until they reach the grubs and inject their eggs directly into the larva's body. Warm and protected, surrounded by its living nourishment, the ichneumon larva has only to let itself live. It first prudently consumes the host's superficial fatty layer, being careful not to attack the vital organs.[22]

OTHER WONDERS

The Interdependence of Things

Another fascinating feature of nature is the *interrelationship* of different organisms, often called an "eco-system." Sometimes they live together in a way that is mutually beneficial. For instance, sea anemones attach themselves to the hermit crab and give protection with their poisonous tentacles. The crabs, in turn, transport the anemones to new feeding grounds...Ants protect, herd, and "milk" aphids in order to obtain honeydew from them...The tickbird removes parasites from the rhinoceros, unafraid of being chomped by the monster...Wasps lay their eggs on bud worms. When the eggs hatch, the wasplets eat the bud worms.

Sometimes the relationship directly involves the food chain.

The ladybird beetle feeds on those aphids that ruin your apple trees and peas...Crop damage is reduced by "friendly" bugs that prey on harmful insects...Bees pollinate crops... "Chairman" Mao (the Chinese dictator) decided that sparrows were a pest and must be eliminated, so he mobilized the populace. Beating on pans, they kept the terrified birds aloft until they dropped to the ground, dead from exhaustion. The extermination continued until a plague of caterpillars destroyed crops and denuded trees. The sparrows were no longer a pest and a nuisance, and Mao ceased meddling with nature.[23]

Ants, together with termites, turn the soil, aerate it, drain it, and enrich it. These good little farmers scatter plant seeds and serve as scavengers, consuming 90% of the dead bodies of small animals.

Polyergus ants can fight but they cannot feed themselves, so they capture slaves to feed them and to do their work.

Camouflage and Mimicry

We are all familiar with the way in which many creatures are colored so as to blend in with their environment and thus make them invisible to their enemies—and also to possible victims. The chameleon is the best-known color-change artist.

Some insects look like twigs, bark, leaves, or thorns. God's endless ingeniousness and originality are astonishing. Men have learned how to disguise personnel, equipment, buildings, and ships in war by the use of camouflage.

Armor

Some creatures are dressed in armor or have other protective devices. The armadillo is covered with a layer of bony plates that are almost impenetrable. The porcupine's quills are painfully effective, as any dog knows that has ever tangled with one. When turtles and tortoises pull in their heads, they are well sheltered. Crocodiles and alligators can be thankful for their tough hides, and even skunks for their repulsive "perfume."

Think of the weapons with which God has equipped His creatures—swords, knives, water guns, and bombs. These are in the form of sharp talons, teeth, tusks, venom, and other chemical poisons. A swordfish can drive its sword through the side of a boat. The bombardier beetle has two sacs in its posterior, containing two different chemicals. When endangered by a predator, it releases these two chemicals into a firing chamber where they are mixed with two other chemicals. The result is an explosive release of hot gas, actually 100° Centigrade or 212° Fahrenheit. Few predators can stand the heat or smell of this smart weapon.

Imagine a fish that can shoot a drop or a stream of water at an insect flying above and bring it down with amazing accuracy. That is the archer fish. In order to perform this feat it must execute a complex equation of geometry and physics, taking into account the distance, direction, and speed of the insect, and the refraction of light in the water. Mind-boggling!

Iridescence

Iridescence is a marvelous play of colors producing a rainbow effect. You see it in the plumage of a peacock and on the neck of a male pigeon. It is all done by the arrangement of the tips of the feathers. Books have been written on the glory of iridescence.

Gravity

Gravitation is a mystery. We can see the results of it but we can't explain it. We know, for instance, that objects fall toward the earth—but why? We know that the moon's gravitation causes the tides on earth—but why? We know so little about it, yet it is the force that, under God, holds the universe together.

The Gulf Stream

I have always been intrigued by the Gulf Stream. Issuing from the Gulf of Mexico, it flows as warm water across the Atlantic without merging with the surrounding cold water. Its influence is felt as far away as Norway, where it raises the temperature along the coast, which is a great blessing to the Norwegians. Don't try to duplicate it in your bathtub; it won't work.

The Water Ouzel

Most of us could live and die without seeing this amazing

creature. If I hadn't seen it myself while on a hike in the High Sierras, I might still be skeptical. It is a small bird, but it has an ability that few other birds have. It can fly down into a mountain stream, walk underwater and feed along the bottom, then surfeited, fly up into the wild, blue yonder again.

Prior Claim

It is no secret that God had a prior claim on many of man's inventions.

Man didn't invent the wheel. The golden wheel spider forms itself into a disk and rolls down sand dunes at 44 revolutions a second to escape its wasp predator. That speed is equivalent to the wheel rotation of a car traveling 200 miles per hour.

It was by studying how a wasp builds its nest, that a Frenchman discovered how to make paper from wood pulp.

Snails carry their own homes with them—the predecessors of mobile homes.

Octopuses and squid move along by jet propulsion.

Beavers, ants, spiders, and bees are adept as architects and engineers.

Silkworm moths made thread long before man did. Birds know how to weave their nests together, as well as to line them.

Female moths broadcast something like radio signals, and the males have receiving sets.

Solomon was right—there is nothing new under the sun!

Busy Bees

When the temperature in a beehive rises enough so that the wax is in danger of melting and the honey in danger of being lost, squads of bees position themselves at the entrance of the hive and beat their wings at a rate fast enough to cool the interior. They can maintain the temperature of the beehive at a constant 94 degrees Fahrenheit, even though outside temperatures vary as much as 60 degrees. Someone has said that their cooling system puts modern air conditioning to shame. Incidentally, the brain of the bee is only about the size of a pin head.

Virgin Birth

Some bees can produce offspring without help from a mate.

It is known as *parthenogenesis,* a form of virgin birth. God makes an exception to His own natural laws and raises a question for skeptics: If certain virgin bees can produce offspring by *natural* birth, why shouldn't a Jewish virgin named Mary be able to do it by *supernatural* birth?

Well-traveled Honey

To produce a pound of clover honey, a bee must visit 56 thousand heads of clover. Since each head has 60 tubes, the bee must dip into three and a third million of them. It may fly as far as eight miles to gather the nectar. Think of the miles flown, the hours consumed, to produce the honey on your breakfast table!

Electricity

Electric eels came before electric stoves. They can discharge 550 volts, enough to stun a man. The African knife-fish produces 300 electric pulses a minute. Some electric fish shock their victims unconscious before devouring them. Fireflies provide light that is 100% efficient; no energy is wasted on heat. You can call it cold light; our fluorescent tubes are unable to equal it.

Underwater Survival

The whirligig beetle carries a bubble of air attached to its tail when it wants to dive into water. The water spider, which lives under water, makes a diving bell of silken sheet, and fills it by transporting bubbles of air.

Avionics

Birds have been experts in aviation as long as they've existed. Some land birds fly over thousands of miles of ocean with no place to land, feed, or rest. They have no way of refueling during the flight. But they build up just the right amount of fat in their systems before taking off. To conserve energy en route, they avoid flying too slow or too fast. They seem to know the optimal speed. And they have to take account of wind resistance. Some birds do this by flying in V-formation.

The blackpoll, a member of the warbler family, flies 2,400 miles from Nova Scotia to South America in four days and nights. The fuel expended for this flight is half its weight.[24]

Think of such fuel efficiency. If your car were that efficient, it could travel 720,000 miles on a gallon of gasoline. It's as if you were just leaving the dealer's showroom with a brand new automobile and he calls after you and says, "Oh, by the way, here's a cup of unleaded gas. It will last you for the life of the car."

There are flying lizards, also known as Draco or flying dragons, which can glide more than 50 feet between trees. Flying squirrels can glide from a high branch to a lower one. The best glider is a sea bird, the narrow-winged albatross, which can soar for hours.

Lures and Traps

Would you believe that some fish, insects, and flowers use lures to attract their next meal? And some have clever traps that snap shut with great precision. The Venus's flytrap has trigger hairs that close the two halves of the leaf when an insect intrudes. And yet an inert substance accidentally falling into the trap would not trigger it. The trap-door spider makes a silk-lined parlor with a silken door. When it senses an intruder nearby, it opens the door, pounces on its victim, and drags it inside.

The Construction Gang

Beavers are engineers of high caliber. They need a pool of deep water in order to build their houses and so they first construct a dam. Using logs and small branches, the little engineers then build their lodge, partly above water and partly below. The lodge has one or more entrances under water. But the beavers must make the entrances deep enough so that they are not blocked by ice in the winter. They store their supply of food in the water near the lodge.

One of the most skilled insect craftsmen is the weaver ant:

> It is one of the very few tool-using creatures in the world. Weaver ants build their nests in trees by joining leaf-edges together. First, several worker ants form a line along one leaf. They then seize the edge of a second leaf, and pull the two together. Another worker approaches, holding in her jaws a larva, or young ant, which secretes a continuous silk thread. While the workers hold the leaves together, the weaver uses the young ant as a tool, moving it back and

forth between the leaf edges until they are held firmly together by a network of silken threads.[25]

If that all happens by chance, then we should worship chance!

Sonar

Bats are noted for their remarkable navigation. They fly in the dark by using a form of echolocation. The pulses of their high-pitched screams bounce back from objects in their path. Dolphins also use this clever method. It is somewhat the same sonar system that sailors use to detect submarines. Radar is different; it uses electromagnetic waves.

Waterproofing

A duck knows how to waterproof itself. If it didn't, it would become water-logged and thus grounded. First it presses its beak against an oil gland near the base of its tail. Then it presses the feathers between its beak, covering them with a thin coat of oil.

Flowers and Vegetation

Every tree, bush, and flower is a wonder of God's creation. The more they are sought out by those who have pleasure in them, the more amazing they are. The oldest living things on earth are the bristlecone pines, on the east slope of the Sierra Nevada range. Some of them are 4,000 years old; they go back to the time of Abraham.

Among the things we owe to trees are fruits, nuts, and oils. From the same soil, they extract nutrients to form apples, cherries, walnuts, and olives. How do they do that? They also provide lumber for building, pulp for paper, and a host of other products. And how often on a sweltering day have we been refreshed by their shade!

Miners in Arizona found the roots of a mesquite tree 700 feet below the surface; the roots had followed what Job called the scent of water (Job 14:9).

What a drab world it would be if we did not have flowers! Jesus said that Solomon in all his glory was not clothed like one of them. The fragrance of some is exquisite. The more closely they are studied, the more beautiful they are, which is more than you can say for *artificial* flowers!

Herbal Remedies

Some vegetation (*serpentina rex*, for example) is useful for medicinal purposes. Pharmaceutical companies send representatives to primitive areas to learn from the nationals what remedies they find in their natural surroundings.

Seeds

Seeds are a wonder. Seemingly dry and dead, they spring to life when given the right combination of water, depth of earth, and sunlight. And their dispersal is a wonder. Some are carried by the wind and water, some by the furs of animals, some by birds, and some by *you*—as you move from place to place with mud caked on your car.

Chemists can name all the elements in a grain and even *combine* those elements— but the result would be *lifeless*.

Pollination

Pollen is carried and deposited exactly where needed by insects, birds, bats, and rain. A bee, for instance, collects it on specially designed areas of its hind legs. Without pollination, we would have no crops.

Atom Vibrations

The National Institute of Standards and Technology in Boulder, Colorado has unveiled an atomic clock that will not gain or lose a second in a million years. It keeps time by counting the vibrations of atoms.[26]

Even Fungi

A fungus that grows in Japan is used to make FK506, which prevents rejection of an organ transplant. And penicillin, of course, is made from molds.

Much, Much More

There's so much more. Birds get new clothes by molting and snakes by shedding their skin. The perfumes of nature are exquisite; it would take volumes to describe them. Birds know *how* to incubate their eggs and *how long*. The hibernation process is a marvel in itself. The hypodermic stings that God has given to creatures—tiny yet ever so effective. The wonders of the Lord leave us breathless!

Conclusion

> *O the depth of the riches both of the wisdom and knowledge of God! How unsearchable are His judgments and His ways past finding out (Rom. 11:33).*

Every work of God is marvelous beyond description. There is nothing God made that does not manifest intricate and perfect design. We are awestruck by the few outstanding examples of His glory that we see in our lifetime, but we see only a fraction of His greatness. There are infinitudes of wisdom and knowledge that we have not explored. For sheer beauty and efficiency, nothing can surpass the work of His hands.

In his book *Critique of Pure Reason,* Immanuel Kant looked out on the world around him and burst into rhapsody. His sentence is inexcusably long (even for a German), but nonetheless worth quoting:

> The world around us opens before our view so magnificent a spectacle of order, variety, beauty and conformity to ends, that whether we pursue our observations into the infinity of space in the one direction, or into its illimitable divisions in the other, whether we regard the world in its greatest or least manifestations—even after we have attained to the highest summit of knowledge which our weak minds can reach, we find that language in the presence of wonders so inconceivable has lost its force and number its powers to reckon, nay, even thought fails to conceive adequately, and our conception of the whole dissolves into an astonishment without power of expression—all more eloquent that it is dumb.[27]

Translation: The creation is so marvelous that it is beyond the power of words or numbers to express, and beyond human thought to take in.

When we consider the order and beauty of creation, it is folly to attribute it all to chance. The variety and design of living creatures say in unison, "The hand that made me is divine." Think of the coordination of the parts of the body, and the marvels of sight, hearing, speech, touch, smell, digestion, memory, dexterity, thought processes, emotions, and heredity.

And then think of the fine tuning of the heavenly bodies, of the just-right composition and density of our atmosphere, of the properties of water, and of the wonder of gravity.

Are we to believe that it all happened by chance, or, as a news magazine reported, "by an amazing biological frenzy." Einstein didn't think so. He said:

The harmony of natural law reveals an intelligence of such superiority that, compared with it, all the systematic thinking of human beings is utterly insignificant.

Sir Isaac Newton didn't think so. His conclusion was: "The most elegant system of suns and planets could only arise from the purpose and sovereignty of an intelligent and mighty Being. He rules them all as the sovereign Lord of all things."

In more recent times, Werner von Braun, noted rocket scientist, said: "One cannot be exposed to the law and order of the universe without concluding that there must be design and purpose behind it all. Through a closer look at creation we ought to get a better knowledge of the Creator."

Sir Fred Hoyle, a British astronomer and a skeptic as well, said that for the first cell to be originated by chance was like saying that a tornado could sweep through an airplane junk yard and assemble a giant jet plane. Harold Morowitz, of the department of Molecular Biophysics at Yale, said that the probability of a single bacterium being formed spontaneously in five billion years is 1 out of 10 raised to the 110th power (translation: infinitely remote).

Other illustrations can be used to show the absurdity of attributing the wonders of creation to chance. It is like taking all the parts of a typewriter, putting them in a washing machine, turning on the switch and waiting until the typewriter is perfectly assembled. Or believing that a tornado could blow through a print shop and assemble the cold type so accurately as to produce a dictionary of the English language. Or throwing bricks randomly and building a palace. Or hurling pieces of scrap metal to the wind to build a sports car.

Even a confirmed evolutionist agreed but refused to accept the evidence. Ernest Kahane, a German biochemist and author of Weltbild der Evolution (World Picture of Evolution) wrote: "It's absurd and complete nonsense to believe that a living cell creates itself; but I believe it, as I can't imagine it happening any other way."[28]

But why this determined drive to rule out God? Man knows that if there is a God, then he is responsible to Him. This idea is completely unacceptable. Man does not want to be responsible to a Higher Power. He wants to go his own way and be his own boss.

Yet in spite of their stubborn clinging to evolution, many scientists stand amazed at the wonders of creation. They use such adjectives as *incredible, wonderful, intriguing,* and *marvelous*. They acknowledge that what they see "should be sweeping us off our feet in amazement."

For those who do acknowledge the Lord as the Originator and Sustainer of creation, His wonders should do exactly that—sweep us off our feet in amazement and draw from our hearts unceasing worship, praise, and thanksgiving. Alex Ross reminds us that:

> The book of the Psalms climaxes with a mighty crescendo of praise to God. The last six psalms add instrument to instrument until, in one final blast, "everything that has breath" praises the Lord (Ps. 150:6). Hear the antiphonal choirs as one generation praises God's works to another (145:4). Listen to the percussion section—"Fire and hail, snow and vapors; stormy wind fulfilling His word" (148:8). And the wind instruments add their notes—the birds and the flowers, the sun, moon and stars. Angels in heaven praise Him, the kings of the earth. Is your voice in there? "Praise *ye* the Lord."[29]

One who has helped untold millions to praise the Lord for His wonders of creation was the father of English hymnody. Isaac Watts wrote:

I sing the mighty pow'r of God
That made the mountains rise,
That spread the flowing seas abroad
And built the lofty skies.

I sing the wisdom that ordained
The sun to rule the day;
The moon shines full at His command,
And all the stars obey.

I sing the goodness of the Lord
That filled the earth with food;
He formed the creatures with His Word
And then pronounced them good.

Lord, how Thy wonders are displayed
Where'er I turn my eye:
If I survey the ground I tread
Or gaze upon the sky!

There's not a plant or flow'r below
But makes Thy glories known;
And clouds arise and tempests blow
By order from Thy throne;

While all that borrows life from Thee
Is ever in Thy care,
And everywhere that man can be,
Thou God, art present there.

PART II

The Wonders of God in Providence

Come and see the works of God;
He is awesome in His doing toward the sons of men.
Psalm 66:5

THE WONDERS OF GOD IN PROVIDENCE

God is not only the Creator; He is also the Sustainer. "In Him all things consist" (Col. 1:17b). He is the One who holds matter together, a fact which incidentally answers one of the problems that still baffles physicists.

As the God of providence, He provides food for all His creatures. The Psalmist said that He opens His hand and satisfies "the desire of every living thing" (Ps. 145:16). Maintaining a universal food chain is no mean accomplishment!

He determines the sex of every baby so that there is a balance in the population of every country.

He directs the course of history. Since He is the Sovereign, it necessarily follows that *history* is "His story." He ordains human governments, sometimes exalting the basest of men. "The king's heart is in the hand of the Lord, like the rivers of water; He turns it wherever He wishes" (Prov. 21:1). He is the divine chess Player, moving the pieces on the board with absolute finesse.

While He is doing all this, He guides all His people in answer to their earnest prayers for light on their various paths.

He protects His people from dangers seen and unseen. Nothing touches them without first passing through a filter of infinite love. "He who keeps Israel shall neither slumber nor sleep" (Ps. 121:4). Someone has said, "We are kept by *the insomnia of God.*"

No evil comes from God, whether illness, tragedy, or death. But He permits these things to happen, then overrules them for

His own glory, for the blessing of those involved, and for the benefit of others. He outwits Satan, demons, and evil men and overrules their wickedness for the accomplishment of His purposes. In that way, He makes their wrath praise Him.

He charts the course of every virus, every germ, every allergy. And at the same time, He controls every spear, arrow, bullet, and missile—even the timing of traffic lights.

Not a sparrow falls to the ground without Him. Such is His perfect knowledge and universal presence. He numbers the hairs of every head. He faithfully ordains day and night, and the seasons of the year. The winds and the waves obey Him; in the words of William Cowper's immortal hymn, "He plants His footsteps in the sea and rides upon the storm."[1]

Our Lord sees that His moral laws are continually operative. For instance, He sees to it that no one can sin and get away with it. He judges evil and rewards righteousness. Sometimes He punishes sin promptly, but more often the wicked seem to prosper (Ps. 37:35). Actually the righteous seem to suffer more than the ungodly in this life. The righteous are not exempt from pain, illness, and trouble. Christians drop dead suddenly, just like others. We should not conclude that accidents and sufferings are always a result of sin in a person's life. When Jesus was on earth, a tower in Siloam fell on 18 people and killed them. Yet He said that the victims were not worse sinners than those who were spared (Lk. 13:4). As Spurgeon said, "The visible providence of God has no respect of persons."

And then there are the spiritual laws of God. He fulfills His promises to the letter. This in itself is an enormous undertaking because the Bible is filled with promises. Someone said that the road to heaven is paved with them.

Nothing escapes His notice, not even the thoughts and intents of the heart. He keeps accurate records. All the works of the unsaved are in His files, and will be brought forth at the Judgment of the Great White Throne. All the works of the believer are there, to be rewarded at the Judgment Seat of Christ. Everything we do for His people is reckoned as having been done for Himself.

It is the Lord who reveals great scientific discoveries to people—not all at once but according to His own time schedule.

And that holds for cures for diseases, too.

The omniscient Lord hears prayer in all languages and answers each one according to perfect wisdom, love, and power. And because He never sleeps, this is going on without letup or interruption. The Lord Jesus not only *hears* prayers; He Himself *prays* for us. And His thoughts toward us are more numerous than the sands of the sea.

He does all these things at one and the same time.

The Bible is one unending record of the providence of God. No matter where you open it, you find the deft way in which He works all things according to His own will. He so arranges circumstances that Joseph rises from a pit to become Prime Minister in Egypt. He guides Ruth to the right place at the right time so that eventually she becomes an ancestress of the Messiah. The story of Esther is filled with plots, sub-plots, counter-plots, and spine-tingling intimations of impending disaster. Yet God foils the enemy and delivers the Jews. What but the interweaving providence of God could shut the mouths of lions in Daniel's day and deliver his three friends out of a red-hot furnace? A tax decree brought Mary to Bethlehem so that Jesus would be born there, in accordance with prophecy. Wicked hands crucified and slew the Saviour, but God overruled their wickedness for our salvation. Divine providence led Philip, the evangelist, to a eunuch who was returning from Jerusalem to Ethiopia. And it was more than coincidence that the eunuch was reading Isaiah 53 when Philip approached his chariot. Out of Paul's imprisonment came four New Testament epistles: Ephesians, Philippians, Colossians, and Philemon. And John's exile in Patmos gave us the fascinating Book of Revelation.

The following are some more contemporary illustrations of divine interventions, of God's arranging things in a way that would never have happened according to the laws of chance or probability. Although these did not all happen at the same time, they *could* have. Similar instances of God's perfect timing and sequence of moves are taking place all the time.

Happy Landing

The time was spring of 1971. The place was Vero Beach, Florida. Billy Graham prayed with his son Franklin and

Franklin's flight instructor, Calvin Booth, before they left to return to Franklin's school at Longview, Texas.

En route they learned there was thunderstorm activity, so they decided to go north to Jackson and west to Longview. This route would take them over several large cities with lighted airports. The original route was over sparsely settled, and hence poorly lit, countryside. As they neared Jackson, the generator failed, leaving them without lights, navigation, or radio. They decided to descend out of the clouds and land at Jackson. Without radio, they couldn't contact the tower. But as they approached, the runway lights went on to full brilliance, the strobes flashed, and a green light signaled them to land.

It wasn't until four years later they found out what had happened. A control tower operator had taken two guests to see how the system functioned. He took a tri-colored flash gun, turned on the red and white lights inside the tower, but for some reason held the gun outside the window when he demonstrated the green light. This would give clearance to any pilot attempting to land. He then demonstrated the runway lights until they reached the state of high-intensity. This would pierce through the fog and clouds for an emergency landing.

When a co-worker then mentioned that an unlighted plane was coming in, the operator said, "There isn't a plane in the air within 50 miles of us." Then Franklin Graham and Calvin Booth landed.

In one sense the operator was demonstrating the system to some friends, but God's providential hand was in it all. Later Calvin wrote, "...it renews our awareness of God's role as guardian of our lives."[2]

A Saint's Doubts Dissolved in Timbuktu

Steve Saint was having a battle with doubts as he traveled in Africa. As he said, he was in a spiritual and emotional desert. He wished he could talk with his father, but Nate Saint had been killed by Auca Indians in Ecuador in 1956. Had his death been a waste? Why did it have to happen? Steve had arrived in Timbuktu on a six-seater plane chartered by UNICEF. But two of their doctors needed seats for the return flight, so Steve might be bumped. How then would he return to Mali?

He tried to hire a truck but was warned that a mechanical breakdown in the desert might be fatal for him. He sought help through the telecommunications office, but it was only transmitting, not receiving messages. Then he remembered hearing that there was a Christian church in Timbuktu. Some youngsters helped him find it, in spite of language difficulties. Next door to the closed church building was a house with a poster. It showed a cross covered by wounded hands, and the words in French, "and by His stripes we are healed." A handsome young man approached, dark skinned and with flowing robes. He quickly found a missionary to interpret and introduced himself as Nouh.

When asked as to his faith in Christ, Nouh told how he had stolen carrots from the garden of a missionary named Marshall. Instead of killing and eating him, as Nouh had feared, Mr. Marshall had given him the carrots, along with some cards with Scripture verses on them. The missionary had offered him a BIC pen if he would memorize them.

After he trusted the Saviour, his mother put poison in his food. He ate the food but was not affected, but when his brother stole a morsel and ate it, he became violently ill and remains partially paralyzed.

Steve said to him, "It can't have been easy for you as a teenager to take a stand that made you despised by the whole community. Where did your courage come from?"

Nouh then told how the missionary had given him some books, and that his favorite was about five young men who willingly risked their lives to take God's good news to stone age Indians in the jungles of South America. The interpreter said, "I remember that story. As a matter of fact, one of these men had your last name."

"Yes," said Steve quietly, "the pilot was my father."

"Your father?" cried Nouh. "The story is true!"

"Yes," Steve said, "the story is true."

When Steve returned to the airport that night, he found that the doctors were unable to make the flight, so there was room for him on the UNICEF plane.

As Steve said, "The whole experience gave me the assurance that God *had* used Dad's death for good. Dad, by dying, had helped give Nouh a faith worth dying for. And Nouh, in return, had helped give Dad's faith back to me."[3]

The Stops of a Good Man

Dr. James M. Gray had planned an ocean voyage to help him recuperate from a long illness. However, when the sailing date arrived, he was smitten with another malady and had to cancel his ticket. Why would God allow this to happen? He sorely needed the change that the trip would have afforded him. H. G. Bosch answers the question:

Soon he received a wonderful answer to his doubting questioning. He read in the newspaper that the steamer on which he would have sailed had struck a reef in St. John's Harbor and had sunk almost immediately! The Lord who had helped him in the past had once again perfectly directed his way and protected him from death.[4]

Was It An Angel?

Ned Meharg and Frank Haggerty had been evangelizing in some remote areas of Bolivia. Late one afternoon they approached a town, pitched camp, and then went into the town to get something to eat. The local hotel had a restaurant but when they went in, the woman in charge said she had no food; she knew that they were *evangélicos*.

Next they went to the police station and asked the desk sergeant if he knew where they might find something to eat. He said, "Sure. At the restaurant in the hotel." But the missionaries explained that they had already gone there and had been turned away. He said, "Come with me," and led them back to the restaurant. There he told the manageress to get these men something to eat. This time she said, "Come back in 45 minutes."

When they returned, she served them deep-fried potatoes and boiled lungs. Both men were hungry, but when Frank tasted the lungs, he didn't like them. So Ned said, "Well, you give me the meat and I'll give you my potatoes."

Soon after Ned began to eat the lungs, his stomach began to burn. He drank glass after glass of water, but the pain only increased. She had put rat poison in the meat.

They had to leave the restaurant and return to their campsite. Ned's condition worsened. Before losing consciousness, he told Frank, "Just send my Bible to my father in Australia."

As Frank was wondering what to do, a tall man appeared. "Your friend is sick, isn't he?" he said.

"Yes, I think he's dying."

"Well you just wait here. I'll be right back."

Soon he returned with an earthenware vessel filled with goat's milk. "Get your friend to drink this," he ordered.

Frank protested that his friend was unconscious.

"Never mind. Force it down his throat."

Frank obeyed, and after some time Ned opened his eyes.

Excitedly, Frank said, "Here, Ned, drink as much of this as possible."

Ned drank and drank and drank. After a while he put his hand on his abdomen and said, "The burning's gone."

Well, the tall man left, Ned recovered, and the next day he and Frank resumed their missionary trek, after leaving some money under the earthenware vessel for their "friend."

Months later, when they returned to that general area, they decided to look for the tall man and thank him. As they told the local people about their mysterious visitor, the folks said, "There are no tall men here." And when they told about the pitcher of goat's milk, the people said, "There are no goats here."

Ned and Frank subsequently shared their experience with a fellow missionary, Dr. Brown from New Zealand. The good doctor said, "The woman put white phosphorus in the meat." Then he added, "The best known antidote for that particular poison is goat's milk."

The Right Place at the Right Time

David Johnson had to return from missionary service in the Philippines with a severe illness that the doctors in Manila had been unable to diagnose or treat successfully. At Stanford University Medical Center, he learned that he had Reiter's Syndrome, which required prolonged treatment. Finally he was ready to return to the work of the Lord.

His flight required a layover in Honolulu. In the airport, Dave recognized an attractive Filipino lady. He went up to her, introduced himself, and gave her a copy of a gospel booklet. It was Imelda Marcos, widow of the late President of the Philippines. If David had not contracted Reiter's Syndrome, he never would have been in the right place at the right time. However, this does not mean that God caused the sickness. He allowed it, then harnessed it for His purposes.

No Free Lunches? Here's One

Richard Varder used to tell about an itinerant tract distributor who had implicit faith that the Lord would provide for his needs as long as he was doing God's will. He agreed with Hudson Taylor: "God's work done in God's way will never lack God's resources." His faith was simple and childlike.

One day, after hours of tract distribution, he was tired and hungry, but unfortunately he didn't have any money to buy food. He believed that in one way or another the Lord would provide. So he went into a small family-style restaurant and ordered a meal. As soon as the food arrived, he bowed his head and silently poured out his heart in unhurried thanksgiving to God. It wasn't one of those self-conscious graces where the Christian nervously scratches his eyebrow!

When he finished, he went to the cash register where the owner was sitting, prepared to give a full explanation of his inability to pay. But before he could say a word, the owner said, "Look here, Dad. When I opened this restaurant, I vowed that the first person to eat here and to ask a blessing on the food should get a free meal. And you are the first such person, so you pay nothing."[5]

However, this incident is not a *carte blanche* invitation for the rest of us Christians to try to get a free lunch! This man was on the King's business and was poor for the kingdom's sake. He was guided by the Lord to do this on one special occasion and had faith that the Lord would provide. Only those who are completely cast on the Lord can expect to see such marvelous interventions. Those who try it under other conditions are tempting God and may wind up having to wash dishes!

The Identifying Verse

Billy B____ was serving the Lord in Bangkok, but he was also serving as a correspondent for two U.S. news magazines.

When he signed a check he always signed it Billy B____, Phil. 1:21. And he always went to the same teller at the bank. One day the teller asked him, "What does Phil. 1:21 mean?" Billy explained that that was his life verse, "For to me, to live is Christ, and to die is gain," and that "Phil. 1:21" was its location in the New Testament, Philippians 1:21.

One night after eating supper in the Oriental Hotel, Billy left in a hurry and forgot his attaché case. In it was his check book, and the check book had a substantial balance because he had just received payment for one of his news articles.

The waiter appropriated the attaché case, filled out a check for a large sum, signed Billy's name, and went to the bank to cash it. Strangely enough he went to the same teller that Billy always used. The teller examined the check and noticed that the signature was a reasonable duplicate. But it was incomplete. Phil 1:21 was missing. The teller called Billy and just as he entered the bank, the waiter fled. Philippians 1:21 had saved Billy a couple of thousand dollars.

God Speaks through His Word

On January 6, 1989, I was doing final page proof corrections on the *Believers Bible Commentary, New Testament*. It was very frustrating [as only computers can be at times]. The computer kept introducing new errors every time a new software conversion was used for typesetting. It seemed that we were facing demonic interference. That morning I received the following calligraphy in a routine mailing from Operation Mobilization:

Don't be frightened by the size of the task. Be strong and courageous and get to work. For the Lord my God is with you; He will not forsake you. He will see to it that everything is finished correctly.
(1 Chron. 28:20, L.B.)

That was just the promise I needed. *"He will see to it that everything is finished correctly!"*

Guided by a Camel Fall and Cholera

Four Christians were traveling in the Middle East, scouting out places for Jewish evangelism. However, Dr. Black had a bad fall from a camel, and it was decided that Dr. Keith would return to Britain with him.

When they reached Austria, Dr. Keith came down with cholera. The Archduchess Maria Dorothea heard of his serious illness and the reason for his travels and promised the protection of the Archduke to any missionaries who might be led to settle there.

A work began among the Jewish people in the city, and among those converted were Dr. Alfred Edersheim and Dr. Adolph Saphir. These Hebrew believers, of course, became illustrious servants of God. God had harnessed a camel fall and a case of cholera to move men on His divine chess board.[6]

Providence, Not Coincidence

Remote is a mild word for describing the place where William and Margaret Rew were serving the Lord. It was in what was then the Belgian Congo. They weren't exactly at the edge of the world, but, as the saying goes, you could *see* it from there! To get food and supplies they had to travel 600 miles. Their shopping trips had to be scheduled in the dry season when the journey occupied three months there and back.

One year they had no funds, so the trip had to be canceled and a long shopping list had to be put aside. However, the Lord had not forgotten them. A caravan of thirteen men arrived, carrying loads which were deposited at the Rew's door. These supplies had been sent by a prospector to whom the Rews had shown hospitality some time previously when he was ill. In gratitude, he decided to buy a year's supply for the missionaries when he was doing some shopping for himself.

The Rew children lived a very Spartan life in those days. They did not always have shoes. But as furlough was drawing near, it was almost imperative that they should have something to wear on their feet. Anna, in particular, was in need. Not to worry! In answer to prayer, a national came to their door to sell a pair of shoes which he had purchased in Elizabethville, 500 miles away. Now he needed money and wanted to sell them. They were a perfect fit for Anna.

Coincidence? No! As F. B. Meyer said, "There is no such word in faith's vocabulary. That which to human judgment is a coincidence, to faith is a Providence."

The Power of a Spider Web

Mark Wheeler tells of a man named Frederick Nolan who was fleeing from his enemies during a persecution of Christians in North Africa:

> Hounded by his pursuers over hill and valley with no place to hide, he fell exhausted into a wayside cave, expecting to be found. Awaiting his death, he saw a spider weaving a web. Within minutes, the little bug had woven a beautiful web across the mouth of the cave. The pursuers arrived and wondered if Frederick Nolan was hiding there; but they thought it impossible for him to have entered the cave without dismantling the web. And so they went on. Having escaped, Nolan emerged from his hiding place and proclaimed, 'Where God is, a spider's web is like a wall. Where God is not, a wall is like a spider's web.'[7]

"Before they call ..."

Jim Haesemeyer, missionary to Honduras, was having a "downer." He should have been happier, the way God was blessing. But he was depressed and discouraged. He admitted that it was crazy. It wasn't natural. This was the only time he had ever experienced depression. After sharing it with his wife, he decided to write to a godly brother in Lubbock, Texas and ask him to pray. When they got to the post office to mail the letter, they found a letter in their box from this very same brother in Lubbock, the first they had received from him in 15 months. Here is what he wrote:

> This is to let you know we think of you often. My writing is a miracle in itself; I haven't even written my own parents. But this evening I truly feel a burden to let you know that we appreciate you and care about you. I know by the Holy Spirit that you find yourself down, but take courage, for our Father will fulfill His purpose in you. Sometimes the hardest part of our walk is just resting in Him ... May our Father richly bless you and your family, answering your requests even before they are spoken.

It had taken 16 days for that letter to arrive from Lubbock. It had been written before Jim had even begun to feel depressed. God's timing was perfect. "Before they call, I will answer" (Isa. 65:24).

In the Nick of Time

It had been an unusually heavy winter. On February 8 there was a blizzard that caused some of the flat roofs to collapse under the weight of the snow. A notorious robber decided it would be a good time to strike. He entered the home of some Christians, ransacked the first floor, then went upstairs to one of the bedrooms where a baby was sleeping. Fearing that the baby would cry and betray him, he carried the little one outside and laid it in the snow. Soon the baby did wake up and cry. This wakened the mother, then the father, who said the crying seemed to be coming from outside. No sooner had they got outside the house than the roof collapsed. Later the burglar was found dead in the ruins, clutching some of his loot. "A Providence that provides for sparrows will surely protect saints."[8]

A Seemingly Chance Remark

It was the Thanksgiving weekend in 1989. David Johnson, Matt Clarke, and I had reached Lone Pine, California on the way home from the Grand Canyon. It was a time of drought, with practically no snow or rain. We committed the day's travel to the Lord before we left the motel. As we sat in a restaurant at breakfast, we saw a car going north with skis on top, and we chuckled. Where did they think they were going to ski in such a time of drought?

After breakfast we planned to drive north three hours to Mono Lake, then cross Tioga Pass to Yosemite and home. As I was paying the cashier, I said, "I guess you're wishing for snow so you'll get some ski trade." She replied, "Funny you should say that. It just came over the radio that it's snowing at Tioga Pass and the Pass is closed for the rest of the season."

We decided to confirm the report at the nearby Ranger's Station. There we learned that *all* the passes to the north had been closed by the snow.

That seemingly chance remark by the cashier saved us six

hours of wasted driving. We drove south, crossed west to Bakersfield, and then straight home.

God's First Class Provision

J. Boyd Nicholson had been on a preaching tour in Zaire and was now returning to his home in Canada. The first leg of his journey was on a small missionary plane to Uganda. Asians there were fleeing the oppressive rule of Dictator Idi Amin, and white persons had just been forbidden to enter. At the airport in Entebbe, the immigration official shouted at Mr. Nicholson to leave immediately. This was impossible; the plane returning to Zaire was filled with missionaries' children. Finally the expulsion limit was extended to 2 P.M. It was leave then or be arrested. The Lord's servant shot up a prayer to the One to whom angels, authorities, and powers are subject.

At 1 P.M., a British plane made an unscheduled stop for fuel on its way to London. The ticket agent explained that every seat was full, but agreed to put Nicholson's baggage on board.

When the passengers were reboarding, the desperate preacher decided to join them. No one asked for his ticket at the door; of course, he had none. Now to find an empty seat!

Seeing his uncertainty, a flight attendant asked for his seat number so he could help find it. But because he had none, he would have to leave the plane. Just then he noticed one seat that didn't have an "Occupied" card. The attendant agreed to check on it, knowing by now that Mr. Nicholson had to leave the country or be arrested.

The wait seemed interminable. Finally the attendant returned, saying, "I don't understand it, sir. We're supposed to be full, but we have to go. That seat is yours."

Soon the plane was airborne. The Lord's servant leaned back in his First Class seat and looked at his watch. It was 2 P.M.

One hour later, when the meal was being served, the crew ran out of steak dinners and asked Mr. Nicholson apologetically if he would take one of the economy meals instead. It was a small sacrifice to make, under the circumstances.

But it proved to be unnecessary. A turbaned Sikh across the aisle explained that he did not eat meat, so an exchange was quickly arranged.

It turned out that Nicholson's fellow traveler was an executive of the airline. Learning of the preacher's dilemma, he assured him of every possible assistance. When they landed in London at 11 P.M., he accompanied the preacher through immigration and customs, then took him to the ticket counter where he arranged for free accommodations in an airport hotel, transport to the hotel, a free breakfast the next morning, and tickets rewritten for Scotland and Canada.

Rehearsing the marvelous providence of God, Mr. Nicholson wrote, "Does the Lord at times smile down upon us, I wonder? Well, that evening, after a luxurious shower and contemplating the comforts of a good night's sleep in a king-size bed, I could not help but smile as I bowed to give thanks to the One who "*...is gone into heaven, and is on the right hand of God; angels and authorities and powers being made subject unto Him.*'"[9]

Extraordinary Texts

Years ago, when W. E. Vine and his brother were in charge of a school in Exeter, England, a call came for W. E. to join the staff of Echoes of Service, a missionary service organization in Bath. Both made it a matter of earnest prayer. One morning when W. E. Vine was having his daily consecutive reading, he came to Deuteronomy 31:7, "Thou must go with this people."

At around the same time, his brother was a guest in a town where he was preaching. After praying in the morning, he rose from his knees and noticed a text on the wall with this unusual combination of verses. "I was left...With good will doing service as unto the Lord" (Isa, 49:21; Eph. 6:7). Later when they compared notes, they were struck by the extraordinary texts, but decided to wait for further guidance.

If the Lord provided an assistant to join the staff, they felt that W. E. would be free to go to Bath. The morning that decision was made, Mr. Vine met a former student of the school and asked casually what he was doing.

He replied that he was working in an accountant's office, but did not wish to continue that occupation and thought of applying for a post as an assistant master; and he added, "You wouldn't have an opening for me, would you?"

This was just the guidance that settled the matter.[10]

Angelic Choir?

It is no secret that just before some believers die, they have a vision of the Lord or of the glories of heaven. Why should we doubt? Before his martyrdom Stephen "gazed into heaven and saw the glory of God, and Jesus standing at the right hand of God" (Acts 7:55).

It has now been revealed that something similar happened when five young missionaries were speared to death by Waorani (*Auca*) Indians in Ecuador on January 8, 1956.

In January 1989—thirty-three years later—Olive Fleming Liefeld revisited the scene of the martyrdom with her husband, Walter. Her first husband, Pete Fleming, had been one of the martyrs.

One day during their visit, Rachel Saint (sister of Nate Saint, another of the martyrs) was talking to two of the Indians who had been present when the men were killed. One had been in the woods and the other right on the beach where the men had died.

Both Indians said they had heard singing. As they looked up over the tops of the trees, they saw a multitude of people surrounded by a hundred bright lights. The lights were very bright and flashing; then they disappeared.

Walter and Olive linked this with the hymn the men had sung the morning before they flew out to the beach where they died: "When passing through the gates of pearly splendor..." Perhaps the martyrs had had a fore-glimpse of that splendor![11]

"Give Us This Day..."

It was during the time when the Japanese had moved into China and had set up internment camps for foreign residents. These camps contained a broad spectrum of business people, teachers, and a few missionaries. Christopher Willis was one of the latter. As he grieved and prayed over the godless conditions in the camp, the idea struck him that he should letter a text of Scripture and hang it in the dining room. Before being interned, he had been able to buy drawing paper, paint, and brushes at close-out prices.

Mr. Willis knew that it was useless to seek permission from the Camp Committee, but he did receive a go-ahead from Mr.

Grant, the chairman. So he lettered a text, five feet long and three feet deep. Early on a Sunday morning he hung it at one end of the room. The text was:

Our Father
Which art in heaven
Hallowed be Thy Name
Give us this day our daily bread

There was mixed reaction to the text. The committee said it must come down because it might be offensive to Catholics and Jews. But the leader of the Catholics said that there was just one thing wrong with the text; it ought to be framed. So Mr. Willis donated a part of his bed with which to make a frame. The Jews said that every word of the text was in their prayer book and that it should stay.

Months later a play was scheduled to be held in the dining room and the text didn't fit in well with the stage props so it was taken down and left in a corner. The next morning at breakfast it was announced that there was no bread. The supply of flour had failed. This continued for three days. Then someone said, "It's because of that text. They've taken down the text, 'Give us this day our daily bread,' and since then we haven't had any bread." Someone else said, "The text is our mascot. We must get it up again." The ones who had taken it down had to put it up again, and then the supply of bread resumed.

After several more months, another play was scheduled and this time the participants hung heavy drapes over the text. Again there was no bread. The yeast supply had dried up. The people murmured about the drapes until those who had hung them were forced to remove them. The bread then reappeared on the tables.

This happened a third time. The text was taken down and thrown behind a piano. The bread failed. A gentleman who had been a brewery manager said to Mr. Willis, "That text should be nailed up so they cannot take it down." Mr. Willis suggested that the ex-brewer handle the matter.

The text remained on the wall until the camp was closed down. The bread supply never failed again.[12]

A Very Present Help

Don Harris was returning from an evening Bible study with five Mexican nationals. He always tried to get home by midnight so that Claire would not lie awake worrying. But this night would be different.

On a lonely stretch of road, the engine went dead and it was only with difficulty that Don was able to steer the car to the side. All the brothers jumped out, looked under the hood, and tried to find the cause. There was a lot of excited talk but no one was able to pinpoint it. Now what? Someone suggested that they get Saulo, an expert mechanic who lived in Zozutla. Good idea! So four brothers started walking to the nearest town, where they hoped to find a believer who would drive them to Zozutla.

As Don waited in the car with Fanuel Montoya, there was little conversation. Just a lot of self-pity that they should find themselves in such a predicament. Then Don broke the silence. "Brother, here we sit with a problem, and we haven't even prayed about it."

"That's right," he answered in rather guilty surprise. "What shall we pray for?"

"Two things. First, that we get the engine problem solved. Second, that we get home by midnight at the latest. I don't want my wife to worry. I always try to be home by that time."

Two hours later the four returned with brother Saulo. He checked the fuel and electrical systems and discovered that the coil was shot. Bad news. No auto parts stores in the area, and even if there were, they wouldn't be open at that time.

Just then a Volkswagen "Bug" passed. Naturally the driver was reluctant to stop, not knowing if these men were *banditos*. He slowed down, did a U-turn about 50 meters ahead, then cruised back slowly enough to check out the situation carefully. He continued down the road, then turned around again, and finally stopped right in front of the helpless believers.

"Anything I can do to assist you?"

Saulo yelled back, "The coil is shot."

With that, the good Samaritan reached over to his back seat, picked up an imported Bosch coil, and handed it to Saulo. An imported Bosch coil was a rarity at that time in Mexico and superior to domestic ones. And for anyone to carry an extra one in his car as a spare part was even more unusual.

Don tried to pay him, but he wouldn't take anything. However, he did accept a gospel tract and was on his way.

The coil was quickly installed and the six grateful believers were mobile again.

Don finally got home at 2 A.M. He tiptoed into the bedroom and found Claire fast asleep. She had dropped off before midnight.

Later, in narrating this incident, Don said, "This was a period in my life when prayer was stale. Knowing my heart, God surely performed this miracle just to remind me that He was still my Friend and a very present Help in time of trouble."

Saved by a Few Inches

Jim was scheduled to preach at a meeting in the boondocks, but he didn't know the way and his car wouldn't start. The battery was dead. So a young believer, Pedro, volunteered to go along in his truck. Everything en route went without a hitch, and the meeting itself was fruitful.

On the return trip it started to drizzle. It had been a long day, and Jim started to doze. He dreamed that he was on a roller coaster, riding crazily. But to his horror he woke to realize it wasn't all a dream. The little truck was spinning around like a top on the wet mountain road. When it hit the side of the road, it started to roll down the embankment—one complete turn, then part of another, leaving the truck lying on the driver's side. When the shock had subsided somewhat and Jim realized he had survived, he also realized that he was lying on top of Pedro. He quickly crawled out through the broken window above him, accidentally kicking on the cab light over the rear window. This enabled him to see Pedro now. His body was inside the truck but his head and neck were outside, with the cab apparently pinning him down. When Pedro shouted for help, Jim was relieved that he was still alive. Immediately Jim tried to lift the car, but he didn't have the strength to do it.

So he ran back up to the road and waved down a passing truck. The driver and Jim now tried to free Pedro from under the truck, but once again, it ended in failure. Pedro was getting increasingly frantic—quite understandably. His cries punctuated the stillness of the scene. He couldn't see anything and was completely trapped.

The next vehicle to come by was a bus. When alerted to the accident, all the men piled out—twenty all told—and ran down the embankment. They were able to lift the truck off Pedro. It was then that Jim got a fresh view of the providence of God. Right next to Pedro's head was a large rock that had cushioned most of the weight of the truck and had saved his life. If the truck had landed a few inches to the left, it would have crushed his head. If it had been a few inches to the right, Pedro's head would have been smashed on the rock. As it was, he escaped with only a broken jaw. Spectators called it incredible luck. Jim and Pedro knew it was the precision of their wonderful Lord.

Cars crashing into one another, cars rolling over, flying glass, twisting metal, and imprisoned bodies, yet God is able to deliver His people while onlookers say, "No one will get out of that wreck alive."

The Still, Small Voice

It happened when Wallace Logan was home on furlough and was staying temporarily in New York. He had a strong feeling that he should visit an elderly Christian lady in New Jersey. The first step was to contact her by phone, but there was no answer, so he concluded that she must be away. Ordinarily he would have dismissed the idea, but a strong impression that he should go remained.

Finally he decided that he should take a train and go to see her. But then the truth crashed in on him that he didn't have the money to buy a ticket. The inner compulsion was so strong that he went to the railroad station and got in line at the ticket counter, a most futile thing to do under the circumstances. There were five people in front of him, then four, then three, then two, then one. At this point a believer from Bethany Chapel in Yonkers passed by and recognized him.

"Brother Logan, what are you doing here?"

The missionary explained that he was going to visit a lady in New Jersey who was well known to both of them.

"Well, let me give you this to buy your ticket," said the man, handing him a $20 bill. (The ticket cost $7.00.)

Mr. Logan caught the train to his destination, walked to the address, and knocked on the door. No answer. He knocked louder. Still no answer. He tried the door knob and found it unlocked. As he opened the door, he thought he heard a moan. Entering he found the lady on the floor. She had fallen and lain there for two days, unable to get up. Mr. Logan called the emergency services and got her off to the hospital, where she made a good recovery.

Obviously God had heard those cries for help from that dear lady and had so influenced the mind, will, and emotions of the missionary to get to her in spite of roadblocks and bring timely assistance.

God's Perfect Timing

Richard De Haan of the Radio Bible Class of Grand Rapids, Michigan, was trying to get back home after meetings in Tampa, Florida. He would first have to change planes in Chicago. All went smoothly until they were over Lafayette, Indiana. There the pilot announced that they would have to "hold" for a while because of bad weather in Chicago. So they "held" for a while.

"Ladies and gentlemen. This is your pilot. Because visibility is zero at O'Hare Field in Chicago, we will have to fly to Atlanta." Checkmate!

Back to Atlanta. Wait in the lounge. Finally, the weather is better in Chicago. On to O'Hare. A good flight and a safe landing there.

Frustration. The flight to Grand Rapids has been canceled. Conventional wisdom at that time is to take a train. No problem. A bus will take him downtown to the train depot. Sure, there is plenty of time.

But that did not take into account the heavy traffic on the freeway. Now Mr. De Haan would never make it to the station in time. And another concern was that his cash was running low.

Tired and tense, he stepped off the bus. Was that someone calling his name? Couldn't be. But it was. Looking in the direction of the caller, Richard saw a good friend who lived a few blocks from the De Haan home.

"What are you doing here?" asked the friend.

"I'm trying to get back to Grand Rapids, and I'm meeting

with nothing but delays, cancellations—you name it."

"No problem. I'm driving home. Why don't you ride along with me?"

Later De Haan wrote, "Did all this happen by chance? Certainly not! The Lord was ordering each step of the way. The next day I learned that the train I had tried to catch broke down just outside of Chicago. How ashamed I was, remembering how I'd complained earlier. Had the bus gone any faster, I would have missed my friend and encountered further delay. Yes, God's timing is always perfect."[13]

Pre-Assigned Seating

John Aker boarded a plane at the Newark, New Jersey Airport. In spite of the fact that the plane was almost empty, he was assigned a seat next to a man named Richard. This man had just been to the Sloan-Kettering Institute for Cancer Research, where he was given ten months to live. For all practical purposes, he was going back to Nebraska to die. It was an ideal chance for John Aker and he seized it.

"May I tell you about something that changed my life?"

Richard nodded.

John explained the way of salvation to him, and asked if he would like to receive the Lord Jesus as his Lord and Saviour.

"Will you trust Jesus for your future—for what lies beyond the grave for you?"

Richard grasped John's hand, and in the clouds above Chicago, he committed himself to the Lord.

Months passed. Again John was flying west from Newark. This time he sat next to an elderly lady. John was astounded to learn that this woman was Richard's mother. Incredible! She was flying to Beatrice, Nebraska. She was a devout believer and joyfully reported that her son was going on well for the Lord. She was encouraged and so was John. How wonderful that the Lord had arranged for John to sit next to Richard's mother.

Then the mother said, "You know, this wasn't my seat. Just before you arrived on the plane a woman asked me to change seats with her and I did."[14]

So many seats on a plane. So many planes. So many flights a day. So many days in the year. Yet God, and not a computer, does arrange the seats. What a wonderful God He is!

Miraculous Provision in the Nick of Time

A pharmaceutical company in Europe offered to send 5,000 IV solutions to Dr. Bob Watt in Nyankunde, Zaire. They were available because there had been a slight labeling error which didn't affect the contents in any way. There was no particular need of them in Nyankunde at that time, but the expiration date was far off, so why not accept the gift?

The journey to Zaire was tortuous. The shipment had to transit Kenya and Uganda. Because of political troubles in Uganda, the border with Zaire was closed immediately after the IV plastic bags had squeaked through. It took nearly a year for the intravenous solutions to reach their destination.

Right at that time a cholera epidemic broke out in the Nyankunde area. Hundreds of patients arrived at the hospital, in danger from dehydration. At a time when nothing could be imported and local manufacture of IV's was impossible, the Lord had provided 5,000 bags—just what the doctors needed.

Looking back on the incident, Dr. Watt commented, "We began to use the precious bags judiciously, and it was like the widow's cruse of oil. While they were needed, we had enough, and when the epidemic was finally brought under control, the last bag was dispensed."

Why Did the Skipper Change His Course?

The desolate seas of Cape Horn were turbulent as the skipper pointed his whaler south into a stiff head wind. He was making little headway and there were no whales in sight.

A thought entered his mind. Why fight the wind? Why not run with it? There are probably as many whales to the north as there are to the south. Why let the waves batter the ship any more than is necessary?

He turned the boat and headed north.

An hour later, the lookout cried, "Boats ahead!" Sure enough, they came to lifeboats with fourteen men on board, the only survivors of a ship that had burned. They had been adrift for ten days, praying for God to rescue them.

Later the skipper said, "I am a Christian. I begin each day

with a prayer that God will use me to help someone. I am convinced that God put into my mind the idea to change the course of my boat in order to save those fourteen lives."

Who can deny it?[15]

Too Close for Comfort

Fred Stanley Arnot and Setobe, his guide, trekking through Central Africa, were forced by circumstances to go hundreds of miles out of their way. The temptation was to chafe at these events, but then Arnot remembered that He was being directed by the One to whom all circumstances are subject—the God of providence.

On the fourth day of their safari, they covered fifteen miles, then stopped at a grove of large trees near a stream of clear water. It had been a pleasant day but they were both very weary. Ordinarily Setobe would have rebuilt the fire to guard against jackals and hyenas. And normally Arnot would have awakened when the night noises of the forest began. But this evening they fell into a deep sleep, utterly oblivious of a danger that was lurking near the very spot where they were sleeping.

Setobe was the first to awaken when the first rays of morning light appeared. As soon as he opened his eyes, he was aware of a deep growling that seemed to come right out of the ground. He continued to listen. Again the wild and terrifying noise began, and chills ran down his spine. By then he was sufficiently awake to notice the pungent smell of animal urine. The seasoned guide knew immediately that there was a lion a few feet away from where he had been sleeping and where the missionary was still asleep.

He crept noiselessly over to the sleeping white man, spear in hand. With one hand he shook Arnot and with the other covered his lips as a warning to make no noise.

Both men stood up and looked around them. Suddenly they were terrified by a deafening roar right near them. They looked down at the ground some four yards from where Arnot had been lying. They could hardly believe their eyes and ears for the roaring that was coming from a hole in the ground. There certainly had not been any roaring when they had retired for the night. As Arnot followed Setobe's careful approach to the edge of the hole, he realized that they had made their camp by the side of a game-pit and that during the night they had inadvertently acted as bait.

On reaching the side of the pit which had originally been covered with small branches, leaves, and grass, they saw that ten feet below was a full-maned lion. He was a fine specimen, and as soon as they peered at him, he began to snarl and roar. It was then they saw that he was unable to move from his crouched position. In the fall he had broken one of his back legs. Having indicated to Arnot that he should stand back, Setobe took careful aim and plunged his spear with full force at the beast's heart. The lion let out a tremendous full-throated roar and began to thrash his body against the side of the pit. The violence of his movements then gradually began to subside and after a few minutes the beast started to emit the inevitable death growls. Setobe lay flat on the ground and leant over the side in order to gain a hold on the shaft of his spear. Having succeeded in this he jerked the weapon free from the lion's body and in the same position he made a second and final lunge as a *coup de grâce.* With a low, resonant moan the lion made one last attacking move with his fore-paw and then collapsed and died.[16]

Bushmen to the Rescue!

Actually, Fred Arnot's life was one unending proving of the faithfulness of the Lord in His providential dealings.

On another safari, Arnot was crossing a desert with Tinka, his guide, and a group of other nationals. The water supply was low. Tinka sensed that the water holes ahead of them would not be adequate because the one at Bukele, usually one of the better supplies, was low.

Breaking camp before dawn, they set out to maximize the benefit of the cool morning. But by midday they were utterly exhausted. The oxen were ready to drop, their tongues hanging loosely out of their mouths. The men decided to unyoke the oxen and lead them to the next water hole, eight miles away. The animals could never have dragged the wagon in that heat.

Only a few drops of water remained in the barrels, and these were rationed out to the men under Tinka's personal supervision. Tinka was in the lead, then Arnot, then a line of dehydrated tribesmen. The heat was unbearable. Even the few gusts of wind were torrid. Every step took a tremendous effort. The soles of the tribesmen's feet were burned, and although Arnot had boots, he felt he was walking on red-hot bars of metal.

Soon Arnot heard the men complaining, but when he tried to tell Tinka, no sound came from his dry mouth. His tongue was bloated and his lips blistered.

Arnot stumbled several times, and on each occasion, Tinka, himself in a sorry state, stopped and gently helped the missionary to his feet. On they went, dragging one foot after the other, closing their eyes for protection against the glare, stumbling, crawling, dragging themselves in the wake of the oxen.

By this time Arnot was too disoriented to pray. The words wouldn't come to his fogged mind. Tinka was like a zombie, and the rest of the men were having a hard time standing. The heat was unendurable.

Arnot remembered seeing the shimmering wilderness before him and the cloudless sky, then he fell to the ground.

For a short time he awoke and saw the black bodies of his entourage prostrate on the ground. No one was moving. He saw Tinka, also flat on his face, with no sign of life. The missionary tried to get up but his feet wouldn't hold him.

With a tremendous effort he pulled himself slowly toward the hunter. His head felt as if it would burst and his throat was so dry that he now found it was difficult to breathe.

Eventually, he reached Tinka who was breathing heavily. He tried to get into a kneeling position and at the same time lift Tinka from the ground but it was no use. He fell forward and lay beside the native, helpless. Again he opened his eyes and saw Tinka's mouth moving. He pushed his face near in an effort to hear what the old man was trying to say. After several attempts, Tinka began to speak.

"Here, too, the water...the w-water is finished, Mon-Monare." He tried to give Arnot a brave smile but collapsed. As the missionary laid his head down in despair, resolved to face the end, he heard Tinka muttering, "M-M-Monare, we...we ne-need...your God n-now."[17]

Arnot began to pray, but the prayer was cut off by unconsciousness.

Now what? Where is your God now, Arnot?

Was it a coincidence that some Bushmen, on a hunting expedition, had drawn near that area when one of them spotted a movement on the horizon? At first they thought it was a herd of antelope, so they set off in that direction with high hopes. But by the time they drew near a clump of thorn bushes, they saw that it was men, who by this time had fallen on the sand. It was obvious that the men were dying, so time was of the essence.

Four of them began digging a cone-shaped hole in the sand, nine feet deep. Sweat poured from their gleaming bodies as they moved furiously on this errand of mercy. Another Bushman cut some reeds and shaped them.

The leader then took a length of reed to the bottom of the cone-shaped hole and pushed it gradually into the ground. After deftly joining a second reed to the first, he began to suck at the end of the second reed. Finally he grinned with satisfaction; he had tasted water. He climbed out of the pit, took a tortoise shell which one of his men handed to him, and descended again. Once again he began to suck. It took several minutes of painful effort, but finally he was successful. The water rose through the reed into the Bushman's mouth and from there into the tortoise shell.

After ten minutes the shell was full of muddy, frothy water. He emerged carefully from the pit, walked over to Arnot, and put the shell to his lips. When there was no response for a while, the others thought that it was useless. But after a while Arnot opened his lips and began to drink greedily. When the shell was empty, the leader returned to his task in the hole.

In that torrid heat, he worked for six long hours until all the men had been revived.

He had worked without pause for the whole of the period and he was exhausted. It was now dark and Arnot's entire party had been succored. The missionary, Tinka, and the rest of the missionary entourage, were now sound asleep. For the first time the leader realized that he himself had not drunk but he was too tired to return to the hollow and his reeds. He remembered the incredulous look of gratitude of the white man and his followers and he smiled before he fell back with his eyes closed and began to snore almost immediately.[18]

The Bushmen arose quietly before dawn, gathered their possessions, and after looking with satisfaction at the white man and his followers, they left the camp. Soon they were chasing a lone bull giraffe.

Eventually Arnot, Tinka, and the rest of the party got up, and remembering the day before, they wondered why they were still alive. Standing beside the missionary, Tinka said, "Monare, I now believe in that God of yours. There cannot be any doubt that we have been saved by His hand. *I* believe...and I shall continue to believe."

Without taking his eyes from the scene Arnot answered, "Yes, Tinka, there cannot be any doubt that it was the work of God."

As he spoke a slight breeze skimmed the top of one of the piles of sand near the water hole and caused the tortoise shell to swivel on its curved back.[19]

The Exact Amount

Arnold Clarke, a missionary in western China, was imprisoned by the Communists after World War II. Upon his release, he was still anxious to serve the Chinese so he went to Thailand. In the mid-fifties, his Volkswagen van began to act as if its condition might be terminal so he decided to get another one of the same model. As he began to ask the Lord for the necessary cash, he added the stipulation that the Lord send the exact amount. Then he would know that the van was the one of the Lord's choosing. There are risks involved in buying a used car.

It wasn't long before he received a check for $3000 from an assembly in the northeast United States. The letter explained that the believers had enjoyed his visit when he was on furlough. Now they had sold a piece of property and wanted to have fellowship with him. The very last statement was, "Maybe you need a car and could use this to buy it."

So he went downtown to look for a van. Sure enough, the dealer had one just like the one Arnold wanted to replace. The price in U.S. currency was $3,256.48. He told the dealer, "All I have is $3,000."

"Well, maybe you could borrow the rest," the dealer suggested.

"No, I can't do that," and he explained to the dealer that he had asked the Lord to send the exact amount.

Unimpressed, the dealer said, "Well, I'd like to sell the car to you, but there are others interested. I'll tell you what I'll do. I'll give you a week to see if you can get the rest of the money."

At the end of the week, the dealer called. "Did you get the money?"

Arnold explained that he had received $254.00. He was $2.48 short.

No problem! The dealer offered to forget the $2.48.

"No, I can't do that," Arnold explained. "I specifically asked the Lord to supply the exact amount."

Mrs. Clarke was listening. She said, "Arnold, I'll give you the $2.48."

But he was adamant. "No, I can't do that."

Running out of patience, the dealer said, "Well, I'll give you three more days to get the money before I give these other people the opportunity to buy the van."

Three days later, Arnold got a large, brown manila envelope from a nine year old girl in New Jersey. She explained that she had heard Mr. Clarke when he preached in her assembly, and that the Lord had laid it on her heart to send her savings to him. Pasted to a piece of cardboard were coins that totaled exactly $2.48. And so he bought the van, assured that he was in the will of God.

Why should we think it is remarkable? Hasn't God promised to guide us if we are walking in fellowship with Him?

An interesting footnote is that the manila envelope had been mailed three months before Mr. Clarke received it. Which means that it was mailed two months before he had started to pray. Our Lord has said, "Before they call, I will answer" (Isa. 65:24).

Very Special Delivery

We have observed God's providences old and new, near and far, large and small. I would like to add another—not spectacular, but nevertheless real and encouraging to me. I experienced it recently in my writing ministry.

On Wednesday, September 15, 1993, I received a fax asking me to send three copies of the *Believers Bible Commentary, New*

Testament, by courier to Novosibersk, Siberia, for potential translators. I was baffled as to how to do it. Then I remembered that my friend, Dave Johnson, was leaving the next night for Moscow. When I called, he was afraid he was already up to the weight limit—but why not try? On Thursday night at the San Francisco Airport we stuffed three copies into his duffel bag with difficulty (these are 1200-page books!). He could barely lock it. In the goodness of God, the ticket agent said nothing about it being overweight. On Friday the books were in Moscow. That is known as *Russian Special Delivery!*

Then the problem was to get the books to Siberia, 2,000 miles away. Dave and Jeff Rittener heard that DHL courier service operated in Russia, so they went to the railroad station to see if they could find a telephone number. It seemed like a fruitless search. Just then they looked out on the street and saw a DHL truck. Dave quickly asked the driver how he could get the books to Novosibersk. The driver said, "Just give them to me." He quickly wrote up the order and promised that the books would be delivered in two days.

Bare Cupboard but not for Long

The Van Ryn family was living in Florida at the time while the father, August, was ministering the Word in Michigan. He thought he had mailed a check to his wife for household expenses, but actually he had put the letter in a coat pocket, then changed suits.

In the meantime, the family till was empty. Mrs. Van Ryn had enough food for the children's breakfast one day but had nothing for their lunch. Without a phone she could not contact August. So she did what she always did; she prayed for the needs of the day.

When the mail came, there was nothing in it to meet the need. So she prayed again, more desperately. At 11 A.M. there was a knock at the door. The delivery man from the local grocery store entered and placed four large bags on the kitchen table.

"What is this?" she asked. "I didn't order any groceries." She didn't explain that she was penniless.

"Well, all I know is that a man came in and bought them for

you. They are all paid for."

"Who was the man?"

"I have no idea. I never saw him before."

After feeding the kids lunch, she made a beeline to the store. The grocer would know. He knew everyone in the neighborhood, and all the people in the local assembly. But when she asked, he assured her he didn't know the man. He could not describe him at all.

So that left Mrs. Van Ryn not knowing who bought them, but knowing very well Who had sent them. The Lord had sent them. When she unpacked the groceries she was amazed. Every one was something that she would have ordered—the same food, the same sizes, and the same brands. What are the odds of some stranger supplying you with the exact same items that you customarily use—the same cereal, cheese, beans, peaches, flour, and butter?

Miracle Tomatoes

You know that expectant mothers often have desires for weird foods or combinations like ice cream and pickles. It seems that their bodies send out signals for elements that are missing at that special time in their lives. But it is true with more than pregnant women. The wife of John Alexander Clarke was seriously ill in Africa. She had a high fever and none of the medicines helped. It would be days before a doctor could reach her. In her weakened condition, she kept asking for a few tomatoes. It was impossible. Neither John nor his wife had ever seen tomatoes growing in that section of Africa.

As her condition worsened, the Christians prayed that her life might be spared. They heard her whispering, "If I only had a few ripe tomatoes."

One day when Mr. Clarke was sitting by his wife's bed, holding her hand, a boy came and announced that there was someone to see him. He resented the intrusion but went to the door to find a national woman carrying a basket with three tomatoes. All she wanted was to know if it was safe to eat these things. She explained that a white man had given her some seed months earlier. Now she had a bumper crop but no one knew if it was safe to eat them. She had just brought these three to show him and would leave them with him.

Well, the tomatoes marked a turning point in Mrs. Clarke's illness. The doctor arrived later with the needed medication.

What a wonderful God we have, interested enough to supply three miracle tomatoes for one of His children.

Meet the Author

Her mission field was London's Heathrow Airport. Day after day, she went there to witness to travelers about the saving grace of the Lord Jesus Christ. Without leaving England she could reach people from most countries of the world. This was her vision, and this is what kept her going. One day in the terminal she sat next to a flight attendant, and struck up a conversation with her. It wasn't long before the Christian lady had made a graceful transition to spiritual matters. The stewardess seemed interested. In fact, it appeared that she was prepared by the Holy Spirit for this particular moment. It was a divine encounter. After hearing a genuine presentation of the good news, she bowed her head and received the Lord Jesus as Lord of her life.

There was still time for our home missionary to drill her on some of the key lessons of the Christian life—the importance of the Word, of prayer, of fellowship with other Christians in a sound church. Then the flight attendant looked at her watch and said, "I'm sorry but I have to go. My flight is leaving in half an hour."

The personal evangelist quickly reached into her literature bag, took out a book by Francis Schaeffer, and handed it to her, saying, "Please read this if you get any quiet time on the flight."

Hours later the stewardess was able to sit in one of the rear seats and start to read. After a few minutes, she noticed a man in the aisle, towering over her. He was looking at the book. Then he asked, "Do you understand what you are reading?"

"Well, I have only been saved a short time and I confess I am having some difficulty with it."

"I see. Then just let me sit next to you and explain it to you. My name is Francis Schaeffer."

Think of the providence of God, arranging for a veteran Bible teacher to come alongside a new believer so that he could explain his own book to her and thus help her along the Christian pathway.

Conclusion

The story is endless. Every moment of every day, our wonderful Lord is working out all things according to the counsel of His own will. He is making the wrath of man to serve Him. He allows Satan and his emissaries a certain amount of rein, then he triumphs over all their evil. What they intend as evil, He works out for eventual blessing to His people. No one can do anything successfully against Him. Frederick Faber said it well:

> *Ill that God blesses is our good,*
> *And unblest good is ill;*
> *And all is right that seems most wrong,*
> *If it be His sweet will.*

Sometimes His providence is seen in miraculous deliverances, sometimes in imprisonment, illness, and death. James is killed by Herod while Peter makes a breathtaking escape from prison. There are times when we cannot trace His hand in the convoluted circumstances of life, but at such times we can always trust His heart. He is working all things together for good to those who love Him. Some day we'll see with clearer vision, and then we will exclaim, "My Jesus has done all things well." In the meantime we can sing:

> *With mercy and with judgment*
> *My web of time He wove;*
> *And aye the dews of sorrow*
> *Were lustered with His love.*
> *I'll bless the hand that guided;*
> *I'll bless the heart that planned,*
> *When throned where glory dwelleth*
> *In Immanuel's land.*
>
> —Anne Ross Cousin

Let's have the great English preacher Charles Spurgeon give us this word on divine providence:

> God's providence is amazing. It staggers thought. It is an idea that overwhelms me—that God is working in all

> that happens! The sins of men, the wickedness of our race, the crimes of nations, the iniquity of kings, the cruelties of war, the terrific scourge of pestilence—all these things are, in some mysterious way, working the will of God. I cannot explain it...I cannot comprehend it. I believe that every particle of dust that dances in the sunbeam does not move an atom more or less than God wishes—that every particle of spray that dashes against the boat has its orbit as well as the sun in the heavens—that the chaff from the hand of the winnower is steered as surely as the stars in their courses—that the creeping of an aphid over a rosebud is as much fixed as the march of the devastating pestilence, and the fall of sere leaves from the poplar is as fully ordained as the march of an avalanche. He who believes in God must believe this truth. There is no standing point between this and atheism. There is no halfway between an almighty God who works all things according to the good pleasure of His own will and no god at all. A god who cannot do as he pleases—a god whose will is frustrated, is not a god, and cannot be a god; I could not believe in such a god as that.[20]

Another Englishman, one who experienced periods of deep suffering in his life, expressed his appreciation of God's providence in the well-known and widely loved hymn:

God moves in a mysterious way
His wonders to perform;
He plants His footsteps in the sea,
And rides upon the storm.

Ye fearful saints, fresh courage take;
The clouds ye so much dread
Are big with mercy, and shall break
In blessings on your head.

Judge not the Lord by feeble sense,
But trust Him for His grace;
Behind a frowning providence
He hides a smiling face.

His purposes will ripen fast,
Unfolding every hour:
The bud may have a bitter taste,
But sweet will be the flower.

Blind unbelief is sure to err,
And scan His work in vain:
God is His own interpreter,
And He will make it plain.

—William Cowper

PART III

The Wonders of God in Redemption

Come and see the works of God;
He is awesome in His doing toward the sons of men.
Psalm 66:5

THE WONDERS OF GOD IN REDEMPTION

Just as God's natural creation is filled with cargoes of wonders, so is His new creation. It will take all eternity to reveal the marvelous work of the Holy Spirit in the lives of men and women, boys and girls, convicting and converting them, making them *new creatures in Christ Jesus*.

J. H. Jowett believes that the wonders of the spiritual creation are greater than those of nature. He writes convincingly:

> The greatest wonders are not in Nature but in grace. A regenerated soul is a greater marvel than the marvel of the springtime. A transfigured face is a deeper mystery than a sunlit garden. To read graces in a life once scorched and blasted by sin is more wonderful than to grow flowers on a cinder heap. If we want to see the real surpassing wonders, we must look into a soul that has been born again and is now in vital union with the living Christ. Even the angels watch the sight with ever-deepening awe and praise.[1]

The varieties of conversion experiences are a wonder in themselves. In one sense, everyone is saved in the same way: by grace through faith in the Lord Jesus and His finished work on Calvary. That is the way of salvation in every age and for all people. And yet the steps leading up to that definite act of faith are as varied as the always unique designs of snowflakes.

Some are saved as adults, some as children. Some are saved from the gutter, some from the cathedral. Conviction of sin comes as a roaring lion to some, but as a nagging pain to others. Some come to Christ the first time they hear the gospel, others after many years of running from Him.

When we get to heaven, we may learn that behind virtually every case of conversion, someone had prayed. It may have been a grandmother who had long since gone to be with the Lord. Or it may have been a mother, still wearing out her knees in supplication for her prodigal son.

When Jesus was on earth, most of the people He helped had come to Him as a result of some crisis in their lives—sickness, blindness, death of a loved one, demon possession, etc. Times haven't changed. It's still our needs that drive us to the Saviour.

Here are some dramatic accounts of conversions that reveal the intriguing variety of the work of the Holy Spirit in conviction and conversion.

The Hippie Who Became Happy

A hippie was crouching in a cave in Palm Springs, wishing he could die. A young man in an old body, he was burned out on drugs, alcohol, and sex. Life was no longer worth living. There was no use going on. In desperation he prayed, "O God, reveal Yourself to me, or I'm going to end it all." Within ten minutes a young, witnessing Christian paused at the mouth of the cave, looked in and saw the moral derelict, and said, "Hi! Mind if I speak to you about Jesus?"

You can guess the rest of the story. The hippie was gloriously converted and left the cave to serve the Saviour. The young man in an old body became a new creation in Christ Jesus.

No one has ever sincerely asked God to reveal Himself without receiving a positive answer. The Lord Jesus promised, "If anyone wills [wishes] to do His will, he shall know..." (Jn. 7:17).

The Sikh Who Sought and Found

Sundar Singh was born into a Sikh[2] family in the Punjab. His mother was a devout woman, but his father wanted his son to succeed in secular affairs. He was not too religious.

The government school was too far away, so Sundar attended the Christian school.

His life came unglued when he was nearing fourteen and

his mother died. From an obedient schoolboy, he became a discipline case, disrupting classes, refusing to read the Bible, and causing trouble on a regular basis. Finally, he transferred to the government school.

He became the ringleader of a gang intent on breaking up the Christian school and driving out the teachers. They stoned the open-air preachers and threw manure when Christian meetings were in progress. Even his father was shocked by the change that had taken place in his son's life.

Brought low with malaria and depression, Sundar asked to be readmitted to the Christian school. He was now more subdued, but was still fighting against God. He and some pals bought a New Testament, took it to his home and burned it. His father rebuked him, saying, "Are you beside yourself to burn the Christians' book? It is a good book—your mother said so."

Finally he came to wit's end corner. If he couldn't find peace, he would commit suicide. After closeting himself for three days and nights, he prayed, "Oh, God! If there is a God, reveal Yourself to me tonight." If he didn't get an answer in seven hours, he would put his head on the railroad track as the next train raced to Lahore.

Before dawn, he rushed into his father's room and said, "I have seen Jesus." The father told him it was just a dream, but he insisted, "No, Jesus came into my room and said in Hindustani, 'How long are you going to persecute Me? I have come to save you. You were praying to know the right way. Why don't you take it? *I* am the way.'"

Then he said, "I am now a Christian. I can serve no one but Jesus."

His father reminded him that only three days before, he had burned the Christian book. Sundar stood rigid, looking at his hands. "These hands did it. I can never cleanse them of that sin until the day I die. But till that day comes, my life is His."

What he didn't know at that time was that the moment he trusted the Saviour, his hands were cleansed of that sin. God would remember it no more.

How Some Bible Critics Were Won

In one way or another, everyone is saved through the revelation given in the Bible. We are "born again, not of corruptible seed but incorruptible, through the word of God which lives and abides forever" (1 Pet. 1:23). If it weren't for the Scriptures, we wouldn't know anything about God's way of salvation. Whether written or spoken, whether a complete Bible or a simple gospel tract, the word of truth figures in every case of salvation (Jas. 1:18).

When Harry Dixon was at Massachusetts Institute of Technology, he had a roommate who was a scoffer. This skeptic would taunt Harry with alleged scientific errors and contradictions in the Bible. Harry sought to answer them, but when they increased in intensity, he finally said, "Here, you are finding fault with the Bible. Have you ever read it?"

The roommate had to admit that he hadn't.

"Well, don't come to me with any more arguments against the Bible until you've had the intellectual honesty to read Paul's Letter to the Romans."

The skeptic accepted the challenge. He read through the letter once and got answers to some of his questions, but he came up with a lot more questions. So he read the letter again, with the same results. And again. And again. When he finally came back to Harry, he was born again. His doubts had been settled and he no longer saw errors and contradictions.

There are other instances of men who set out to disprove the Christian faith and who ended up as loyal followers of the Saviour. Lord Lyttleton and Gilbert West teamed up to show that everything supernatural in the Bible was false. With his keen legal mind, West set out to prove that the resurrection of Christ was nothing more than a legend. And Lyttleton would write a companion book showing that the conversion of Saul of Tarsus was a mere myth.

This meant that they had to read the Bible carefully, which neither of them had done, according to their own admission.

The more they studied, the more their positions were shaken. The final outcome was that they wrote classics *defending* the Christian faith. Gilbert West's book was *The Resurrection of Jesus Christ,* and Lord Lyttleton's was *The Conversion of St. Paul.*

Something similar happened to Frank Morison. Although he had a reverent regard for Jesus Christ, he was an unbeliever. He had serious doubts concerning the Gospel records. So he decided to write on the last seven days of Jesus' life. Only later did he realize that the days following the crucifixion were just as crucial.

His book *Who Moved the Stone?* is a treatise on the truthfulness of Christ's resurrection. The first chapter, referring to his original intention, is entitled *The Book that Refused to be Written.*

Not so well known is the story of Lew Wallace. When the vociferous skeptic Robert Ingersoll challenged him to write a book proving the falsity of Christianity once for all, the ex-governor of Arizona began to gather resource material at home and abroad, determined to publish the masterpiece of his life and the crowning glory of his work.

After writing four chapters, it became clear to him that Jesus Christ was a real Person after all. Wallace was in an uncomfortable position. Gradually he came to see that Jesus was the Person He claimed to be. He wrote:

> I fell on my knees to pray for the first time in my life, and I asked God to reveal Himself to me, forgive my sins, and help me to become a follower of Christ. Towards morning the light broke into my soul. I went into my bedroom, woke my wife, and told her that I had received Jesus Christ as my Lord and Saviour.

"O Lew," she said, "I have prayed for this ever since you told me of your purpose to write this book—that you would find Him while you wrote it."[3]

Wallace continued to write, and his masterpiece was the novel *Ben Hur, a Tale of the Christ.*

The Weather Vane that Pointed to Christ

Sometimes people find the Lord when, to all appearances, they aren't even looking for Him. That was the case with Peter Jenkins. Hiking across the country, he had reached Mobile, Alabama. There a friend invited him to what was to be a really wild party. He felt tempted to go, but he also saw an ad about an evangelistic campaign, and he was curious about that. He had never gone in for that sort of thing. He ridiculed it as "Jesus joinin'." But now he found his soul spinning like a weather vane, and it finally led him to the James Robison Crusade.

Sitting in the front row of an auditorium holding 10,000 people, Peter felt a little foolish about being there, but satisfied himself with the excuse that he would be able to take some pictures.

Then the preacher took his place behind the podium and thundered out the gospel. The tall, tough Texan impressed Peter "more like a linebacker for the Dallas Cowboys than a preacher." But the message of Calvary's Cross was going out, and the Spirit of God was working. Finally the invitation was given. Repentant sinners were invited to come forward and accept Jesus as Lord and Saviour.

About 300 people moved forward. Peter asked himself, "Is that me standing there among them?" Yes, it was! As Robison asked the people in front of the podium, "Will you accept Jesus as your personal Saviour?" Peter's lips moved. "Yes, I will." He meant it.

Robison went through the words again, asking the people to signify their acceptance of Christ. Peter reconfirmed his decision. Later Peter wrote,

> Relaxed and clear-eyed and more inwardly at peace than I had ever been, I floated out of there and back into the street. I never did get to that real wild party. I had gone to a realer and more far-out party than any I might have missed.
>
> Like a wavering compass needle that points at last to north, that weather-vane soul of mine had found the direction it would point to from now on. Now I knew what folks meant when they talked of 'amazin' grace.'

From Pearl Harbor to Paradise

Who would ever have thought that the Japanese pilot who led the attack on Pearl Harbor in 1941 would one day become a believer? Or who but God could ever have devised the steps that led to it?

Mitsuo Fuchida was his name. Jubilant at having struck such a heavy blow at the U. S. Navy, he radioed the news of the victory back to Tokyo. The outlook for his country in the Pacific was definitely favorable.

But then America awoke like a slumbering giant and mobilized to counter-attack. Before long Japan was on the defensive, then finally defeated in the ashes of Hiroshima and Nagasaki.

Captain Fuchida was furious. He determined to bring the United States before an international tribunal and try it for war crimes. In order to do this, he prepared to collect stories of atrocities committed against his fellow-countrymen.

He began with those who had been held as prisoners of war in the States. But instead of hearing of crimes, he came across a recurring story of an American woman who visited the men in internment camp. She brought them candies, cookies, and a little book called the New Testament. They were caught off balance by her kindness. When they would ask her, "Why are you treating us like this? After all, we are your enemies," she would always reply, "It's because of a prayer my parents prayed before they were killed." Her parents had been Christian missionaries in the Philippines. When the Japanese invaded, they executed the parents, but not before the couple had lifted their hearts to God in prayer. Now the daughter explained her kindness as springing from that prayer, but she never told the Japanese prisoners what the prayer was.

This was hardly the kind of evidence that Mitsuo Fuchida was looking for! He wanted accounts of war crimes. But the story kept repeating.

One day Mitsuo obtained a copy of the New Testament. He was curious. He read the Gospel of Matthew but was not particularly struck by it. He read Mark's Gospel, but once again he was unmoved. But when he came to Luke 23:34, he read, "Father, forgive them, for they do not know what they do." Without help from any person, he knew immediately the prayer that those missionaries had prayed before they were put to death.

Mitsuo Fuchida promptly repented of his sins and trusted the Lord Jesus Christ as his Lord and Saviour. Until his death in 1969, he traveled in many countries, proclaiming the unsearchable riches of Christ and the way of peace with God.

The Words that Wouldn't Die

God is long-suffering, not willing that any should perish. He stands at the heart's door in sunshine and rain, patiently waiting to gain an entrance. Sometimes His patience extends over many years. Dwight L. Moody illustrated this with an unforgettable example.

One night he had preached on Matthew 6:33, "But seek ye first the kingdom of God, and His righteousness; and all these things shall be added to you." At the close of the meeting, a man came up to him in extreme agitation.

"Mr. Moody," he said, "when I was leaving home, my mother pled with me to trust Christ but I said, 'I can't think of that now. I have to go out and make a living.' But I promised her that I would go to church every Sunday.

"When I settled in my new accommodations, I found that my mother had put a Bible in my bag with Matthew 6:33 marked, 'But seek first the kingdom of God and His righteousness, and all these things shall be added to you.'

"On the first Sunday, I went to church. The preacher took as his text Matthew 6:33. I thought it was more than a coincidence. I wanted to trust Christ but I didn't do it. I slipped out.

"The next Sunday I went to a different church. The text that day was Matthew 6:33. I knew that God was chasing me down. I knew that He was speaking to me. I was greatly stirred. But I said I would come to Christ some other time.

"Some weeks later I was in another town. Would you believe it? — the minister spoke from Matthew 6:33. Some people sitting near me questioned me and found that I wasn't saved. They urged me to receive the Lord Jesus. But I said, 'No, if I did that, I wouldn't be able to do what I want to do.' And so I went out, rejecting Christ.

"Mr. Moody, I have attended church for forty years. I wanted to keep that promise to my mother. But in all those forty years, I have never heard that text again.

"Then tonight I came into your meeting and you preached on Matthew 6:33, 'But seek first the kingdom of God and His righteousness, and all these things shall be added to you.' Mr. Moody, do you think that God will still forgive me and save me?"

Moody assured him that the door of salvation was still open, and that night the penitent entered in. God's patience had extended over forty years, and a mother's prayers had followed for that long, too.

Incredible Coincidence

Sometimes we have to smile at the divine ingenuity. God works in ways that make reason dizzy. We might be tempted to doubt this story by George Cutting if we didn't know him to be a man of unquestioned honesty and integrity, a man not given to exaggeration or embellishment. Many of us know him through his writings, especially the gospel tract, *Safety, Certainty, and Enjoyment.*

One day he was walking down the street of a small English village when he had a distinct impression that he should call out, "Behold! The Lamb of God who takes away the sin of the world." To all appearance there was no one within earshot, and it seemed so foolish to do it. But Cutting was in touch with the Lord and near enough to hear the voice of the Holy Spirit. So he quoted John 1:29 out loud.

Then he had an impression that he should repeat it, and he did.

Six months later, he was doing door-to-door evangelism in that village. When he asked a lady in one cottage if she was saved, she assured him joyfully that she did indeed belong to the Saviour.

"How did it happen?" he asked.

She told him that six months previously, she was in deep conviction of sin. There in her little cottage, she cried out to the Lord for help. Right at that moment, she heard the words, "Behold! The Lamb of God who takes away the sin of the world."

She said, "Lord, if that's You speaking, say it again." And again she heard the wonderful words, "Behold! The Lamb of God who takes away the sin of the world." That morning the burden of her sin was lifted and she entered into peace and joy through faith in the Lamb of God.

What a wonderful thing to be a man like George Cutting who is sensitive to obey the promptings of the Holy Spirit, even if they seem preposterous![4]

Unconventional Evangelism

Thomas Bilney was an unprepossessing fellow who used to go to hear Hugh Latimer. Although "Little Bilney" wasn't much in the eyes of men, he knew God, he knew his Bible, and he had a good measure of spiritual discernment. He had great affection and appreciation for Latimer, but as he listened to his sermons, he sensed that there was something seriously missing. The messages appealed to the intellect but not to the spirit. They were scholarly but not life-giving. Latimer was sincere and earnest, but he was not saved. Bilney cried to God for some way in which to reach him. He longed to be the instrument of his illumination.

The opportunity came one day when Latimer was coming down from the pulpit.

"Father Latimer, may I make my confession to you?"

Latimer naturally expected a confession of sin. Instead, Bilney confessed his faith in Christ. He told how he had found peace through 1 Timothy 1:15: "This is a faithful saying, and worthy of all acceptation, that Christ Jesus came into the world to save sinners; of whom I am chief."

Latimer is taken by storm. He is completely overwhelmed. He, too, knows the aching dissatisfaction that Bilney has described. He has experienced for years the same insatiable hunger, the same devouring thirst.

To the astonishment of Bilney, Latimer rises and then kneels beside him. The Father-confessor seeks guidance from his penitent! Bilney draws from his pocket the sacred volume that has brought such comfort and rapture to his own soul. It falls open to the passage that Bilney has read to himself over and over and over again. "This is a faithful saying, and worthy of all acceptation, that Christ Jesus came into the world to save sinners, of whom I am chief."

The light that never was on sea or shore illumines the soul of Hugh Latimer, and Bilney sees that the passionate desire of his heart has been granted him. And from that hour Bilney and Latimer lived only that they might unfold to all kinds and conditions of men the unsearchable riches of Christ.[5]

It was that same Bishop Latimer who was later burned at the stake for his faith in Christ. The same one who, just before his death, said to his fellow martyr, Bishop Ridley, "We shall this day...light such a candle in England as shall never be extinguished."

Sledgehammer Evangelism

Another example of unconventional evangelism took place in Holland in later years. Dr. Abraham Kuyper graduated from the University of Leiden with honors in theology. His spiritual life was cold and lifeless, just like the church life of his day. When he began to minister in a small church in Beesd, he encountered vital Christianity for the first time. The simple folk there were living demonstrations of the power of the true Christian faith. One Sunday after his sermon in that country church, a woman accosted him and, with unusual candor, said, "Dr. Kuyper, that was a fine sermon, but you need to be born again." The arrow struck home. Kuyper abandoned his false profession, turned himself over to Christ, and went on to become an eminent preacher, educator, devotional writer, and statesman. For four years he served as Prime Minister of Holland.

From Atheism to Christ

Although raised in the Anglican tradition, C. S. Lewis turned to atheism as a teenager. His education at Oxford was interrupted by military service in World War I. Still a convinced atheist, he returned to Oxford to study philosophy and English literature.

When he was 24, his no-God philosophy began to experience some set-backs. He formed an instant friendship with Neville Coghill, the most intelligent and knowledgeable student in his class and a man of outstanding character. Lewis was disappointed when he learned that Coghill was an out-and-out Christian. This happened with several other friends—they were extraordinary men in every respect, except that they were believers.

And this same thing happened with authors whom he valued—men like George MacDonald. He considered it a pity that MacDonald had to be a Christian. Lewis looked on Gilbert Chesterton as the most sensible man alive, but he too had embraced Christianity. Many others had the same imperfection.

God, his Adversary, had begun to work on Lewis's intellect, emotions, and will. As he realized later, the great Fisher of men was playing His fish, and the hook was already in Lewis's jaw.[6]

Or, to change the figure, the "Hound of Heaven"[7] had started to chase him and would not let him escape.

His atheism suffered some telling blows, but He still refused to acknowledge God as God. He grudgingly spoke of Him as Spirit. Even *that* was a big concession. After all, he must not make a complete surrender! He must be able to maintain some measure of pride.

Through reading Chesterton's *Everlasting Mind,* he came to admit that Christianity made sense—apart from its Christianity. This was a curious contradiction, a kind of illogic that his stubbornness forced on him.

In 1926, the most hard-boiled of his atheist friends admitted the possible historicity of the Gospels. He confessed that the story about the dying God must have actually happened once. As God continued to close in on him, Lewis was shattered.

It was during this time that he experienced conviction of sin. In his own words, "I found what appalled me; a zoo of lusts, a bedlam of ambitions, a nursery of fears, a harem of fondled hatreds. My name was Legion."[8]

In 1929, alone in his room at Magdalen College, he felt "the steady, unrelenting approach of Him I so earnestly desired not to meet."[9] Then and there he acknowledged that God is God. He knelt and prayed, "the most dejected and reluctant convert in all of England."[10]

Looking back on that experience, he marveled at "the divine humility which will accept a convert even on such terms." He asked, "Who can duly adore that Love which will open the high gates to a prodigal who is brought in kicking, struggling, resentful, and darting his eyes in every direction for a chance of escape?"[11]

From that moment when he first admitted that God is God, he moved on to the great doctrines of the Christian faith. One morning he set out on a trip, still denying that Jesus Christ is the Son of God. When he arrived at his destination, he believed. At last he found the joy that he had been seeking but couldn't find in atheism.

Lewis' conversion is an illustration of Spurgeon's observation that the history of the Church of God is studded with the remarkable conversions of persons who did not wish to be converted, who were not looking for grace, but were even opposed to it, and yet, by the interposing arm of eternal mercy, were struck down and transformed into earnest and devoted followers of the Lamb.[12]

Saved by Overhearing the Gospel

Yes, the seeking Saviour finds the lost sheep in unusual ways. Sometimes when a soul winner is explaining the way of salvation to one person, a listener for whom it is not intended is converted. This happened at a Naval Air Station in Hawaii. A sailor was witnessing to a buddy at the corner of the hangar. Another sailor, standing unseen around the corner, heard the message and believed. As far as we know, the one to whom it was directed did not.

No Longer Hell Bound

Erik was brought up without religious training but he had a little playmate in the neighborhood who used to tell him Bible stories that her mother told her. This was his first brush with the Bible. In high school, someone used to leave Chick tracts around, i.e., tracts that presented the gospel in cartoon format. As Erik read about hell, he would murmur to himself, "I don't want to go there."

Once when he was walking in a mall with his brother and sister, a young lady accosted them and asked, "Have you heard the word of the Lord?" His brother and sister walked on, ridiculing the girl, but Erik stopped to hear what she had to say.

Soon life became a nightmare of drinking, drugs, burglaries, and trouble with the police. He enlisted in the Navy, but that didn't last. He bought a classic motorcycle in his search for satisfaction and arranged for an artist to paint a picture of the devil on the side—horns, tail, pitchfork and all—and to letter the words HELL BOUND. Those words were an apt choice because Erik raced crazily around the city, trying to impress his girlfriends with death-defying stunts.

He decided to reform and attend a community college. A fellow-student used to invite him to a Bible Class on campus, but he always had an excuse. Then one day he decided to go. The lesson that day was on hell. Erik was shaken. At the close, a young man (who later became one of Erik's elders) led him to Christ.

He determined that he should sell the motorcycle, but all efforts were fruitless. When he shared his frustration with a fellow believer, the latter asked, "Erik, now that you're a Christian would you sell a motorcycle with HELL BOUND on it?" Erik confessed that he had never thought of that. So he went to work to see if he could remove the picture of the devil and the words that went with it. To his amazement, he was able to do it so smoothly that the original surface was the same as when it came from the factory. He knew by this that the Lord was working in his life. There was another way by which he knew—someone bought the motorcycle the next day, paying the full price that Erik listed. No longer *hell bound,* Erik was now *heaven bound.*

Caught Off Guard in Gibraltar

Spurgeon tells of two soldiers who were on guard duty in the long underground passages of Gibraltar. One was a decided Christian; the other was experiencing deep soul trouble. They were quite a distance apart in a long corridor where sounds reverberated. "The soldier in distress of mind was ready to beat his breast for grief; he felt he had rebelled against God, and could not find how he could be reconciled."

The other sentinel, at the far end of the corridor, was meditating on the redemption that is in Christ Jesus. Suddenly he was startled when an officer came out of the darkness and asked him for that night's password. In his confusion, the soldier blurted out, "The precious blood of Christ." Then he quickly recovered and gave the proper word. But in the meantime, the words had winged their way to the other end of the passageway and reached the soldier who needed them.

Spurgeon says that the words had passed along the passage and reached the ear for which God meant them, and the man found peace with God, being in later years the means of completing one of our excellent translations of the Word of God in the Hindi language.[13]

Won Without a Word

We often hear of people coming to the Lord as a result of the life of a believer. Drunken husbands have turned to Christ because of the submissive lifestyle of their Christian wives. The fact that it still works is shown by the experience of Bert Graves at a military installation.

After hours, he often joined other fellows in basketball games at an outdoor court. Unknown to him, he was being closely watched by Dick Kegler. Dick noticed that Bert didn't lose his temper, that his speech was clean, that he was consistently fair.

One night Dick approached him and said, "Bert, you're different. You have something I don't have. I don't know what it is, but I want it."

Bert graciously explained that it wasn't an "it;" it was a Person, and His Name is Jesus. Dick was ready. He closed in with God's offer of salvation that evening.

The Unsolved Case of a Stolen Bible

God's trains always run on time, but some trips last for years. Some conversions are simple; others are the result of plot and counterplot, of wheels within wheels, an amazing movement of men on God's chessboard.

Years ago, C. Ernest Tatham and two other young men had been having evangelistic meetings with A. H. Stewart in New Brunswick. Each morning Mr. Stewart met with his team after breakfast. He would take his Bible, a gift from the popular preacher H. A. Ironside, and conduct a Bible reading in Exodus. On September 2, he wrote in the margin, "We finished reading Exodus today in Campbellton, New Brunswick."

After Mr. Stewart returned home to Guelph, Ontario, a burglar broke into his car and made off with his bags—including his most treasured earthly possession, his Bible. The police investigation was fruitless; the thief was never caught.

Eight years later, Ernie Tatham was conducting meetings in a place far removed from Guelph. We are going to let him take up the story at this point.

"'Have you heard what's happened to Wilbur McNaughton?' Little Mrs. Harvey looked straight into my face at the close of that country church meeting. 'And who is Wilbur McNaughton?' I asked with a smile. 'Oh, I thought that you probably knew him. Most of the folks in these parts do. Anyway, he's been converted, and what a change,' she beamed.

"'You know,' she went on, 'he was never much for church. In fact, whenever he goes on a drunk, everyone is scared of him. But now—it's wonderful—he has become a Christian, and he's a new man. And guess what? He found the Lord through reading a big Bible that a fellow gave him. Someone had given it to this fellow but he didn't want it himself and so passed it on to Wilbur.'

"Before leaving the church, Mrs. Harvey promised that she would try to get Wilbur out to one of the special services.

"Sure enough, he showed up one evening the following week. When I met him, I said, 'I hear that you've trusted Christ. Is that correct?'

"Wilbur smilingly confirmed this. He told how a friend had given him a Bible and that he started to read it. Because his wife was uninterested and even hostile, he usually did it secretly. As he continued reading, his interest deepened and his heart became increasingly hungry. Late one night, when he was reading John 14, the Lord Jesus seemed to reach out to him, beckoning him to trust Him with his very soul. He seemed to hear Jesus' voice and to see His wounded hands. For the first time Christ became real to him, and he yielded himself to the Lord, spirit, soul, and body. Alone in his room that night, he became a genuine, born-again Christian. He would never be the same again.

"Noticing that Wilbur was holding a large Bible under his arm, I asked if this was the Book that he had been reading. He said that it was and passed it to me. I could see that many of the pages had handwritten notes and comments. As I thumbed through the pages, my heart quickened. At the end of Exodus, I read, 'We finished reading Exodus today in Campbellton, New Brunswick.'

"My heart began to race with amazement. I could scarcely believe my eyes. 'Look at this,' I cried. 'I was with A. H. Stewart in New Brunswick the day he penned this comment.' The friends around me gasped and shook their heads.

"The next day I called Mr. Stewart and enjoyed hearing his shout of astonishment and joy. He had despaired of ever finding the Bible that had been stolen. But now, years later, in a village 150 miles away from his home, the Bible reappeared, having been God's sovereign instrument in leading a lost man to Jesus Christ as Saviour. There was only a remote chance of its ever being retrieved. And I was probably one of the only two or three people on earth who could positively identify it.

"On learning the full story, Mr. McNaughton tearfully returned the precious Book to its owner, and received a fine replacement in return."

How unsearchable are His judgments and His ways past finding out (Rom. 11:33b).

Another Bible That Wouldn't Die

When W. P. Mackay was leaving his Scottish home, his mother gave him a Bible which she had inscribed to him on the flyleaf. She had also added a verse of Scripture.

In time the young Mackay became an ardent infidel and adopted a lifestyle that was consistent with his atheism. He sank ever lower into alcoholism and extreme forms of immorality. At one time he pawned the Bible in order to buy liquor.

In spite of his dissolute behavior, he became a successful physician; in fact, he rose to be head of the largest hospital in Edinburgh.

One day he was on duty when a patient arrived who had been horribly mangled. Dr. Mackay was amazed by the man's peace and radiance. At first the doctor tried to reassure him that all would be well. But when the patient demanded to know how long he had to live, the physician said, "Three hours at the most."

To the doctor's amazement, the man said, "I am ready. I'm saved and I'm not afraid to die. I will go to be with the Lord Jesus." Then he asked if someone could get a certain book for him from his landlady.

Dr. Mackay sent an orderly for the book, then started on his rounds through the hospital. But the man's calm assurance rattled him. He couldn't get it out of his mind.

Later he returned to the ward and asked the nurse how the patient was doing.

"He died just a few minutes ago."

"Where is the book he asked for?"

"It's under his pillow, right where he put it."

As the doctor reached under the pillow, he brought out a Bible. It fell open to the flyleaf and there he saw his own name, his mother's name, and a verse of Scripture. It was the Bible his mother had given him when he left home for college, and which he had pawned.

Mackay rushed with the Bible to his office, fell on his knees, and asked God to have mercy on him. He repented of his sinful life and received Christ as his Lord and Saviour.

In later years, he wrote a book called *Grace and Truth,* and preached the good news of salvation to multitudes.

The Conquest of Addiction

Chris started out drinking. He was invited to a three-day party, and desperately wanted to fit in with the crowd. But peer pressure almost cost him his life that night. He was rushed off to the hospital to be dried out.

He began to sell and use marijuana. Then some of his friends advised him to quit fooling around with that small stuff and get into cocaine, where the big money was. He soon built up a brisk business, selling half a pound each week. And he started using it heavily himself.

One day when he was "stoned," he went to his parents' house and was terrified to see the whole place filled with police. He rushed into the bathroom and flushed $17,000 worth of cocaine down the toilet. Then he took out his knife, brandished it at his father, and ordered him to get those police out of the house. Actually there *were* no police in the house. Chris had a king-sized case of paranoia.

At another time, he flushed $10,000 worth of cocaine down the drain, then tried to take his own life. When he was released from the hospital he was flat broke, so he went back to his parents' house. In the meantime, his brother Mark had become a believer. Chris saw a change in him, and when Mark invited him to a Bible Class, he felt strangely drawn, and so accepted. Ordinarily he would have had no inclination or intention to be there. After the class, an older lady known as "Grandma" started to talk with him. As she did, the other people quietly left the room. He thought, "That's funny. What's going on here?"

First Grandma took him to 1 John 5:13. She suggested that he put his own name in the verse. When he did so he learned that when Chris believed in the Name of the Son of God, he could know that he had everlasting life. In Ephesians 2:8 he saw that salvation is a gift. That all he had to do was accept it and thank the Giver. That night Chris passed from death into life. Not only that—he passed from addiction to freedom in Christ.

A Ten Dollar Promise

An evangelist met a farmer and said, "Fine day, isn't it?"

The farmer replied, "It is indeed. It's a great day."

"I hope you thank the Lord for His mercies every day before you leave your home. You *do* pray, don't you?"

"No sir, I don't. I never pray. I've got nothing to pray for."

"That's strange. Does your wife ever pray?"

"She can pray if she wants to."

"And your children. Don't they pray?"

"There's nothing to stop them from praying if they so desire."

The evangelist said, "I want to make a deal with you. I will give you ten dollars if you promise that you will never pray as long as you live."

The farmer agreed, pocketed the ten dollars, and congratulated himself for getting the money so effortlessly.

But that night he began to think about the deal. "What have I done? I've promised that I would never pray. No matter what problem or sorrow or crisis comes, I must not pray. When it comes time to die, might I want to pray then? I will have to stand before the Judge, and maybe I'll wish then that I had prayed."

The more he thought about it, the more troubled he became. His misery increased as he thought about the weight of sin that was burdening him. His wife could see that he was in deep soul trouble, so she asked him what was bothering him. Finally he told her about his promise that he would never pray. She said, "The devil tempted you and you have sold your soul for ten dollars!" That thought drove him to distraction—so much so that he was not able to work for several days.

The evangelist was having meetings in the neighborhood and rather expected the man to come. Sure enough, he showed up one night. The preacher's text that night was Mark 8:36: "What will it profit a man if he gains the whole world, and loses his own soul?"

At the end of the meeting the farmer rushed forward with the ten dollars in his hand. Stretching it forward, he cried out, "Take it back. Take it back!"

"What's the matter?" asked the evangelist, "You wanted the ten dollars and you said you didn't need to pray."

"But I must pray. If I don't pray, I'm lost."

Soon he was on his knees, crying out to God for forgiveness and for salvation.

The sovereign Spirit had arrested another sinner and made him a member of the family of God.

An Unlikely Verse Answers an Absurd Objection

Sometimes we have the idea that God can save people only through verses of Scripture that are solidly evangelistic, such as John 3:16, John 5:24, and Romans 10:9. On the contrary, every word of God is living and powerful, and He can use the most unlikely passages to bring light to darkened souls.

J. Oswald Sanders told of a blind Christian who had tried for a long time to lead an elderly lady to the Lord. He had tried every approach he could think of. He had used all the well-known gospel verses. He had brought in vivid illustrations of how substitution works. All his efforts were fruitless. She just couldn't seem to see the truth.

Before visiting her one day, he told the Lord how unsuccessful he had been in the past. He said, "Lord, I can't go on anymore unless you give me some passage of Scripture to share with her." As he was praying, the following verse jumped into his mind: "And you shall be my sons and daughters, saith the Lord Almighty" (2 Cor. 6:18b). He couldn't understand how a verse like that could have anything to do with a person's salvation. After remonstrating with the Lord, he found that no other verse would come, so he told the Lord he would use it.

He explained to the woman how he had run out of ideas in order to get the gospel across to her. He had told her all he knew. So he had asked the Lord for a verse, and he quoted it: "And you shall be my sons and daughters, saith the Lord Almighty."

"Does it say *that* in the Bible?" she exclaimed.

"Yes, but why do you ask?"

"Well, all the other verses you gave me were about *men*. 'Him that cometh to me I will in no wise cast out.' 'He that heareth my word.' Does it mean *women* too? Does it include *daughters* as well as sons?"

After telling the story, Sanders commented, "Who but the Holy Spirit could ever have helped the woman out in this way? She had an absurd objection, yet a soul-winner who depended on the Holy Spirit, received from Him the verse that brought salvation to her."

And then he added, "How dependent on the Holy Spirit are we?[14]

A somewhat similar case involved a young woman whose passion was dancing. She was never more happy than when she was on the dance floor. Evening after evening, she glided over the floor in the arms of her friend. What more could life afford than this?

Then it happened. One night in the middle of a dance, a verse from Jeremiah flashed into her mind. She had learned it as a child in her home. It was not what we commonly think of as a gospel verse. But Jeremiah 2:13 came with convicting power into her heart: "For My people have committed two evils: They have forsaken Me, the fountain of living waters, and hewn themselves cisterns—broken cisterns that can hold no water."

She was shattered as the truth broke on her in convicting power. She was forsaking the Lord for entertainment that did not satisfy permanently and had no eternal value.

She left the dance floor and never returned to it. Her life was transformed, and she lived to tell forth the excellencies of Him who had called her out of darkness into His marvelous light.

Mel Trotter, A Trophy of Grace

Mel Trotter was a remarkable fellow in many ways. He inherited an Irish gift of gab from his father and had a way of ingratiating himself with others. But he was a bartender as a boy and a drunkard at 17. No wonder disaster dogged so much of his life.

Trotter loved excitement, he loved to be with people, and he wanted freedom to do as he pleased. Always clever, always charming—and *almost* always drunk.

He decided to learn to be a barber, where there would be plenty of chance to talk while he was cutting. But liquor got an ever-increasing hold on him. The chains of addiction wound themselves around him, and his frequent resolutions to go straight always ended in failure.

During one of his few periods of sobriety, he married a lovely young lady, but it was only after several months that Lottie realized she had married a drunkard.

Mel was fired from his job and decided to sell insurance. Then he and Lottie had the joy of welcoming a baby son into the family. Again Mel tried to straighten out, and he moved his family to a house in the country, eleven miles from the nearest saloon. His best resolves collapsed. One night he was so desperate for a drink that he traded his horse for some whiskey at the saloon. He had to walk home in freezing cold, but this sobered him. By the time he reached the house he was full of good intentions.

After moving to Davenport, Iowa, he went steadily downward. He would be away from home for days at a time. After disappearing for ten days, he returned home shaking and miserable and was met by a brokenhearted Lottie. She broke the news that their baby had died that morning.

Mel was crushed by sorrow. At the open casket of the baby, he promised to Lottie, to God, and to the dead baby that he would never take another drink. That afternoon, two hours after the funeral, Mel Trotter staggered home dead drunk.

A story persists that he took the shoes off the baby in the casket and pawned them for a drink.

Lottie promised the Lord to serve Him in any way she could, and she covenanted to pray for Mel and to keep on believing that somehow God would make Mel His own.

In the months that followed, he disappeared entirely. He drifted aimlessly from town to town, begging, stealing, and selling his shoes for the price of a drink.

He drowned in shame and guilt, blaming himself for the death of his son. The promise he had made haunted him.

Barefoot and disheveled, he arrived in the Chicago freight yards in freezing January weather. Painfully he made his way to the streets, panhandling for enough money to buy a few drinks.

One saloon keeper bounced him out, calling him a barefoot bum and suggesting he walk east to Lake Michigan until his hat floated. As he staggered along the sidewalk, probably on his way to Lake Michigan, a small man with a bushy head of curly hair took him by the arm and led him through the door of the Pacific Garden Mission. Mel slumped into a chair and went to sleep immediately, leaning his head against the wall. After leading the audience in a hymn, Harry Munro called on the men to pray for the broken wreck of humanity that had just come in the door.

Later, Mel woke sufficiently to know that he was in a religious meeting. As Harry boomed out the gospel, the words began to sink into Trotter's consciousness. When Harry gave an invitation to accept Christ, the first man to raise his hand was Mel Trotter. At 9:10 P.M., Harry and Mel knelt at the old, worn altar, and Mel asked the Lord for forgiveness and received Christ as his Lord and Saviour. A new name was written down in glory.

It didn't take long before Lottie learned that her prayers were answered.

Her husband lived to become the Superintendent of the Pacific Garden Mission, then later established the Union Rescue Mission in Grand Rapids, Michigan. He also had part in founding 67 other rescue missions in this country. And he became one of the most powerful evangelists of his day.

One of his favorite sayings was: "One thing God never remembers, and that's a confessed sin. One thing God never forgets, and that's an unconfessed sin."[15]

Forgiven[16]

Menda Turner had stayed up all night, waiting for her husband to return in his pickup truck. He had been out, preaching the gospel in the surrounding territory. He had always made it a point to return on time so that his wife would not worry. But this night he never came home.

Search parties were sent out in the morning, and they found the pickup overturned in a ditch by the side of the road. Mr. Turner's body was lying in the middle of the road, stripped naked. Everything belonging to him had been looted. It was a tremendous blow to Menda. She had come to love the African people, and now it seemed that when her husband was in an accident, some of them would either pass by or, even worse, would loot the accident scene. All the errands he had collected in the Copper Belt were gone.

The natural thing for Menda to do would be to return to her home in England, but she was made of better stuff. She decided to continue serving the Lord right there in Zambia. So she poured out her life, caring for hundreds of destitute, starving, and dying refugees from Angola that passed through her area. She became known as Mama. Her place was flooded with needy people.

Fifteen years passed. One day her kitchen boy announced that a man had come to see her. When she went out, she saw a tall, strapping African. He wanted to speak to her privately, so they sat down in chairs on the veranda. But soon he got up, knelt down, put his hands on her feet, and said, "I have something to confess to you." He said, "Fifteen years ago, your husband was killed and his body and car were stripped. I know that the word got around that it was an accident, but it wasn't so. Mrs. Turner, I was one of four men who murdered your husband. I have now been saved by the grace of God and am soon to be baptized and received into fellowship in my local assembly. I felt I should come back to you because I couldn't go and be baptized until I had received your forgiveness. I don't know where the three others are, but I know I have to confess to you. I am guilty of your husband's death. Can you please forgive me?"

The whole scenario of her husband's death passed before her, the disappointment she had felt in the African people she loved. There was the added trauma of knowing that he had been murdered by the African people for whom she and her husband had labored so faithfully and lovingly. It hurt very much. Now a man was kneeling before her with his hands on her feet, confessing the murder, and saying he wouldn't get baptized unless she would forgive him.

Menda Turner, an ordinary English housewife, had the character of a spiritual giant. And she had a heart for the Africans. She closed her eyes, thought for a moment, then took his hands off her feet, held them in her own hands, and said, "How can I not forgive you for what you have done when God has forgiven me for being part of a world that murdered His Son. Yes, I forgive you." She had taken seriously the words of the Lord Jesus, "Forgive and you shall be forgiven." She realized that she had been forgiven an enormous debt she could not pay. Now she found the grace to forgive the repentant murderer of her husband.

In due course, she retired and returned to England, and recently she went into the presence of the Lord. Hers surely must have been an abundant entrance into the everlasting kingdom of our Lord and Saviour Jesus Christ.

Teresa's Testimony[17]

Teresa was a cultured Spanish lady who migrated to Mexico during a time of political upheaval in Spain. She had been trained by nuns and was determined that nothing would change her beliefs or her church. Her life was filled with trials, but these did not bring her closer to the Lord. They only hardened her.

From her expensive apartment, she looked down on a row of hovels in the backyard where people lived in abject poverty. This was a great offense to her, because she was a very refined person. But there was one family that particularly attracted her attention. She knew that the husband worked at the docks. She could see that they ate miserable food for a family of six, but they always gave thanks to the Lord and sang some songs before eating. She was very impressed by this.

As the months went by, she got to know them better and they lost no time in witnessing to her concerning the Saviour they loved. After a while they irritated her and she told them she didn't want to hear any more. She was a Roman Catholic and would always be a Roman Catholic.

Soon Doña Teri moved to another location, glad to get away from these people who were witnessing to her about the Lord Jesus. But Don Roberto found out where she was living, and it wasn't long before he was knocking on her door and testifying about the Saviour. For seventeen years, this family followed her and told her about the One who would save, keep, and satisfy her. But she steadfastly refused. She went to confession and mass faithfully and refused to bow the knee to the Lord Jesus.

Finally she accepted an invitation to visit the assembly when she learned that a refined Argentinean was going to speak. She was impressed by the singing and by the friendliness of the people, but most of all by the Word of God which she heard. When she went home that night, she made an inventory of her life, what had happened to her, what satisfaction she had received from her belief in the Roman Catholic church. She decided that what she had really been looking for was an experience with the Lord Jesus and she accepted Him that night.

Soon she began testifying to her neighbors, those on the left and those on the right. She let them know that the Lord was *numero uno* in her life. In time both of these families came to know the Lord, and the blessing overflowed to their relatives. The web was working and a large group of people was added to the assembly.

Zachariah Finds the Saviour[18]

Zach was a student at a technical college, intent on getting a diploma but also intent on draining the cup of pleasure at the same time. He knew that there was a person named Jesus Christ, but he had no understanding of the claims of that great Person on his life. In a dream one night, he saw a woman across the table from him. The only thing she said was, "I have a message for you." Sometimes when we dream we can't remember the subject, but this time he couldn't forget. Her words haunted him.

When he went down to breakfast the next morning, the girl in his dream sat opposite him at the table. He was so startled by this that he rose from the table, left the breakfast, and went out of the dining room. At lunch time the same girl sat across from him. This unnerved him so much that again he left his food and exited the dining room. The same thing happened again in the evening. It happened again the next day for the fourth time. Now he couldn't sleep, let alone eat. His friends began to worry about him. They asked him to point out the girl to him so that they could talk to her and find out why she was harassing him.

The girl's name was Susan. She was a member of a nearby Christian assembly. When Zach's friends spoke to her, she was completely ignorant of the problem. In fact, she hadn't even noticed Zach. All she could say was, "I don't know who you're talking about and I don't know why he's upset." They explained the dream to her and asked what it was she wanted to tell him. Obviously she had a message for him. She was mystified by this. She said, "The only thing I can think of is that I'm a Christian and maybe God is trying to speak to Zachariah." They said, "If we bring him to your room, will you tell him the message you have so that he can start eating again?" Susan agreed, still wondering what was going on.

His friends brought Zach to her room. He was somewhat hesitant to come, but with the encouragement of his friends he agreed. Susan opened her Bible and presented to him the story of the Lord Jesus Christ, of His willingness to save anyone who would put his trust in Him. Zach was so sure that God had spoken to him in this unusual way that he, on the spot, confessed his sins and received the Lord Jesus as his Lord and Saviour.

Lost and Found

He belonged to the restless generation. He had to get away from home, from the establishment, and from familiar surroundings. So he decided to leave Toronto and head out for Edmonton, Alberta. He didn't know anyone there, but a friend had given him the address of his father, a farmer in Red Deer. His strategy was to get some outdoor work, make a lot of money, and then head back to Ontario with all his problems solved.

When he reached Edmonton, someone stole his suitcase with all his belongings except what was on his person. So he searched out the highway to Red Deer and started walking. A farmer took him in and provided room and board. But after two weeks Greg hit the road again toward the Crowsnest Pass. As he walked along, a young fellow and a companion stopped and shouted, "Are you looking for a ride?" At that time, Greg wasn't hitchhiking, but the fellow persisted, "Well, get in anyway and

I'll take you to the next town." En route the driver asked, "Do you have a place to sleep?" Greg admitted that he didn't, so the fellow said, "Well, you meet us at the hotel tonight and we'll take you to our cabin in the woods."

True to his word, he was there at the end of the day to pick Greg up. He shared the cabin with these two fellows. Before they went to bed, they read their Bibles. Greg thought this was strange but it didn't particularly unnerve him. He liked to think he was open-minded, having dabbled in Eastern mysticism, Transcendental Meditation, and New Age philosophies.

In the morning Greg went back to town to look for a job, contracting a chill on the way. There was no work for him, so he went back to the cabin, intending to pick up his few miserable belongings, then head out. But when he reached the cabin, he was very sick and he had to stay in bed for two or three days with pneumonia.

A kindly man named Blair visited from time to time. It was only then that Greg learned that he was at a Bible camp, and that Mr. Blair was the manager. As he regained his strength, Greg worked around the camp and took his meals with Mr. and Mrs. Blair. They talked to him about the Lord but did not in any way pressure him to make a profession of faith. After a week, he thought he should leave but felt strangely constrained to remain. So he asked the manager if he could stay and work in return for room and board, and his offer was accepted. As the camp sessions started, he heard the gospel message, unaware that the Christians were fervently praying for him.

Nearby was a motel, owned by Christians. They offered him work, and this kept him under the sound of the gospel. By now, he was under great heart pressure. He asked questions like, "Is the Bible true?" and "Is Jesus really God?" The believers answered him as best they could. The conviction of sin increased. He made a mental chart, listing the pros and cons of becoming a Christian and of not becoming a Christian. Finally he decided to take a day off, go up the side of the mountain and not come down until his decision was made. But he never got to the mountain. When he reached a field about 100 yards from the motel, he threw himself on the grass, gazing up into the heavens. There he realized that he really needed Christ and the forgiveness of sins that He offered. In a simple prayer he repented and asked Christ to save him. He got up, feeling that a great burden had been lifted and that he was soaring.

Back at the motel, the Christians noticed a change in his countenance. The frown was gone, replaced by smiles. But they said nothing.

Two days later, he publicly confessed Christ at the camp, causing great rejoicing to erupt there. Soon thereafter he returned to Ontario, a new man in Christ Jesus, anxious to share his Saviour with his family.

Think of the divine coincidences. The theft of his suitcase. Being picked up by a Christian when he wasn't really asking for a ride. Being taken to a cabin at a Bible camp, of all places. Being forced to remain there because of pneumonia. Thus hearing the gospel day after day. How great are God's judgments and His ways past finding out!

Abdel, the Muslim

What made Abdel an unusually devout Muslim was that he claimed to know the entire Koran by heart. When he happened to come to a Christian youth hostel in Israel, he found that there were a few Muslims there. He didn't want them to hear the Christian message, so day after day he would come and ask distracting questions. He also had the unpleasant habit of blowing smoke into the teacher's face, a great irritant.

That wasn't all. When the leader would seek to answer the questions, Abdel would just look around, completely uninterested in what was said. It was obvious that his only purpose was to disrupt the ministry of the hostel. After about three weeks of this, the teacher had to travel to England and he quickly forgot the frustration caused by Abdel.

But something happened to Abdel. He lost his flat, and one night as he slept on the beach, he had a dream. He heard himself asking all the questions that he had voiced, but, even more, he heard all the answers, exactly as they had been given. Then everything fell into place. There on the beach at 2:30 in the morning, he accepted Jesus as his Saviour. The teacher had been long gone, but the Holy Spirit had continued to work. It was a great breakthrough, and Abdel became a powerful testimony for the Saviour. This was living proof that God's Word will not return to Him void, but will accomplish what He has sent it forth to do. And it shows that the message is more important than the messenger. The messenger was no longer there, but the message was in Abdel's mind and eventually reached his heart.

Ahmed, the Jordanian

Ahmed was also a Muslim. He was a Jordanian motorbike police officer who had crossed over into Israel when the border was opened. Eventually he made his way to the Christian hostel mentioned previously. Day after day, he sat and watched the Christians. Eventually he picked up a Bible in Arabic and read the entire Old Testament in five days. At the end of that time, a Jewish believer shared with Ahmed how he had come to acknowledge Jesus as his Messiah. First his mother was saved, and she began to pray for her family. Then the father, son, sisters—all the family came to the Lord and became Messianic believers. But he also told him how they had been neglected and rejected by the Jewish community because they believed that Yeshua (Jesus) was the Messiah. Ahmed responded, "If I shared with my family and friends that Jesus and not Mohammed is the promised Messiah, then they might kill me."

For days Ahmed counted the cost of taking his stand for Christ. During those days he told how he had changed from hating the Jews to loving them because he had met some of them at the hostel. Finally he made the great decision to receive the Lord Jesus as His Lord and Saviour. A week later he asked to be baptized, publicly confessing his faith before the world. Then he returned to Jordan to tell his three wives and all his friends about the living, loving Saviour.

He illustrates the truth of 2 Chronicles 16:9: "The eyes of the Lord run to and fro throughout the whole earth, to show Himself strong on behalf of those whose heart is loyal to Him."

Where Can I Find the Messiah?

The story of Leopold Cohn is a familiar one. A European rabbi, he had been reading Daniel 9. When he came to verse 26, it was clear to him that the Messiah would come before Jerusalem was destroyed. Since Jerusalem was destroyed in A.D.

70, the Messiah had already come. He hastened to an older rabbi and asked, "Where can I find the Messiah?" It is commonly reported that the rabbi replied rather flippantly, "Go to New York. You can find anything there." Well, he did go to New York. There he wandered the streets searching for the Messiah. One day he heard singing as he passed a meeting hall. Inside he heard the good news of salvation, and found the Lord Jesus as his Messiah and Saviour. He purchased a horse stable, cleaned it thoroughly, and began to hold gospel meetings. That was the beginning of a very fruitful ministry.

History has a way of repeating itself. A taxi driver in Israel had the good fortune to pick up a fare who was a committed Christian. The believer challenged him to go home and read Daniel 9 and Isaiah 53. Well, he accepted the challenge. When he got off work, he went home and read both chapters. In Daniel 9:26, he read, "And after the sixty-two weeks Messiah shall be cut off, but not for Himself; and the people of the prince who is to come shall destroy the city and the sanctuary." To him it seemed clear that the Messiah would die before the city of Jerusalem was destroyed. Since the city was destroyed by Titus in A.D. 70, it followed that the Messiah had already come. As a result, he realized that God had visited His people Israel.

Without delay he bought a copy of the New Testament and began reading it, asking the Lord for a definite sign that the Messiah of whom the Christians spoke was the real one. He expected the New Testament to be an anti-semitic book. But in Matthew 5 he saw the blessedness of the book, and in chapter 11 the care of the Messiah-Jesus for His people. He read and read and read, and after about two weeks he came to the end of the book of Revelation.

Now is the time to pause and mention that this man had been a paratrooper in the war. He had fought in some of the great battles, including the capture of Mount Hermon, and had seen twelve of his buddies killed. As a result, he had so hardened himself that he hadn't been able to weep for fifteen years. But when he came to the end of the New Testament, something happened that he did not expect. His hardened heart was softened, as it is written in Ezekiel 36:26: "I will give you a new heart and put a new spirit within you; I will take the heart of stone out of your flesh and give you a heart of flesh." As his heart softened, he began to weep and weep and weep. The tears flowed for hours. He realized that God had loved His people, and had given His unique Son to die for His people and for the people of the world. He also realized that his tears and his softened heart were the sign for which he had asked. He repented of His sins and received Jesus as his Messiah-Saviour.

Still a taxi driver, he now witnesses to his customers whenever the opportunity presents itself. He loves to speak of the resurrection of Christ as the only hope and consolation for Israel.

Johan's Story

Meet Johan, a Hollander, brought up in a Bible-believing home. Due to a series of financial reverses, he became the breadwinner in the home. But the pressure was too much for him, and he landed in a hospital with a bleeding ulcer that required surgery. The doctor took his father aside and said, "Look, your son was made for freedom. Let him go." It was a strange thing for a doctor to say, but it was true. Johan wanted freedom more than anything else. But he was convinced that Christ and freedom could not exist together. So he began to travel.

Eventually he came to the desert in Israel, near the Red Sea. He built a small hut near the city of Eilat. At night he looked at the stars and came to the realization, "Yes, there is a Maker." He was amazed.

One day he was sitting in the shade, watching the ships sail by. He thought, "That's it. If I could just see the world, I would be satisfied." Just then a stranger came and sat beside him. Strangely enough, he too was a Dutchman. Johan shared how he longed to sail around the world to find satisfaction. The man said, "I have been around the world twice and there is no way out of that circle. It doesn't satisfy. But I have found the purpose of living. I have found One who does satisfy and His Name is Jesus. I was a Catholic and I never looked at the Bible. But someone gave me a King James Bible and I started to read it. There I came to the truth in Jesus Christ." When Johan looked into John's eyes, he felt he saw reality. He learned that John had been saved only a month previously.

That night Johan decided to decorate his hut. He thought a

world map would be good, so he reached into his back-pack to find one. Instead he found a Bible that his mother had placed there. One of the verses that jumped out at him was Galatians 5:1, "Stand fast therefore in the liberty by which Christ has made us free, and do not be entangled again with a yoke of bondage."

It was after a period of time that Johan realized that he had had the wrong focus. He was concentrating on freedom rather than on the right Boss. So he repented of his sins and received the Lord Jesus as His very own. Interestingly enough, John and Johan subsequently have been serving together in the desert for over 23 years, telling anyone who will listen of the One who has called them out of darkness into His marvelous light.

Conclusion

We grant that the conversion accounts presented here have been dramatic and unusual. But it is also true that every genuine case of conversion is a supernatural, miraculous work of the Holy Spirit. He is innovative, unpredictable, and resourceful—and He never repeats Himself.

Believers who were brought up in a Christian home and who were protected from the world's contagion often feel disadvantaged. They consider their testimonies to be tame and colorless by comparison. It would be wiser for them to rejoice over the guilt and shame they have been spared, and to realize that they are just as truly trophies of grace as Paul, the apostle. Every conversion experience is interesting and memorable.

What staggers the imagination is that our great God, at one and the same time, and in all places, is influencing the intellects, emotions, and wills of people, seeking to lead them to repentance and faith. His methods are original and unpredictable. He is putting together the parts of millions of puzzles, ever populating heaven with sinners saved from every tribe and nation. The full story will be the subject of eternal amazement and of endless worship. What a wonderful God we have!

This wonderful God is praised in a still popular hymn from the 1700's, written by Samuel Davies:

Great God of wonders! all Thy ways
Are matchless, God-like, and divine;

But the bright glories of Thy grace
Above Thine other wonders shine.

Refrain:
Who is a pard'ning God like Thee?
Or who has grace so rich and free?

Such deep transgressions to forgive!
Such guilty sinners thus to spare!
This is Thy grand prerogative,
And in this honor none shall share.

In wonder lost, with trembling joy,
We take the pardon of our God:
Pardon for crimes of deepest dye,
A pardon bought with Jesus' blood.

ENDNOTES

PART I

[1] Charles Haddon Spurgeon, *Treasury of David* (Grand Rapids: Baker Book House, 1983), V:209.

[2] Excerpted with permission from "How Color Affects Your Moods and Health" by Lowell Ponte, *Reader's Digest*, July 1982. Copyright 1982 by the Reader's Digest Assn., Inc.

[3] Edmund Bolles, *Remembering and Forgetting* (New York: Walker and Company, 1988) p. 139.

[4] Quoted by Mark Looy in "I Think: Therefore There is a Supreme Thinker," *Impact*, October 1990, San Diego: Institute for Creation Research, p. 2.

[5] Roger Penrose, "Those Computers Are Dummies," *Time* Col. 135, No. 26, June 25, 1990, pp. 74-75.

[6] Isaac Asimov, "In the Game of Energy and Thermodynamics You Can't Even Break Even," *Smithsonian Journal*, June 1970, p. 10.

[7] Drs. Don DeYoung and Richard Bliss, "Thinking About the Brain," *Impact*, February 1990, p. 1.

[8] Jerry Bergman, "Mankind—the Pinnacle of God's Creation," *Impact*, July 1984, p. 2.

[9] William Hartston, *The Kings of Chess* (New York: Harper & Row, Publishers, 1985), pp. 47, 71.

[10] Spurgeon, *Treasury of the Bible* (Grand Rapids: Baker Book House, 1983), I:305.

[11] Stuart E. Nevins, *Planet Earth: Plan or Accident,* Impact #14, pp. 1-4.

[12] Helga Menzel-Tettenborn and Gunter Radtke, *Animals in their Worlds* (New York: Grosset & Dunlap, 1972), p. 29.

[13] Ibid., p. 56.

[14] Ibid., p. 165.

[15] M. R. DeHaan II, *Our Daily Bread,* June 8, 1991.

[16] David C. Egner, *Our Daily Bread,* April 15, 1991.

[17] Menzel-Tettenborn and Radtke, *Animals,* p. 297.

[18] Michael E. Long, "Secrets of Animal Navigation," *National Geographic Magazine,* June 1991, p. 76.

[19] J. Sidlow Baxter, *Awake, My Heart* (Grand Rapids: Zondervan Publishing House, November 1978), p. 36.

[20] Adapted from "Creatures of the Namib Desert," National Geographic Video, narrated by Burgess Meredith, 1977.

[21] Adapted from *The Living Planet: The Northern Forests,* Time-Life Video, narrated by David Attenborough, 1987.

[22] Menzel-Tettenborn and Radtke, *Animals,* p. 233.

[23] *Time Magazine,* December 28, 1992, p. 76.

[24] Michael E. Long, "Secrets of Animal Navigation," *National*

Geographic, January 1991, p. 76.

[25] Lucy Berman, *Nature Thought of It First* (New York: Grosset and Dunlap, 1971), p. 83.

[26] *USA Today*, April 23, 1993, p. 1.

[27] Immanuel Kant, "The Critique of Pure Reason," *Great Books of the Western World*, Encyclopedia Britannica, Inc., 1952, XLII:187.

[28] Quoted in "If Animals Could Talk" by Werner Gitt and K. H. Van Heiden, Christliche Literatur-Verbreitung e.V., Bielefeld, Germany, 1994.

[29] Alex Ross, "Choice Gleanings Calendar," August 2, 1991.

PART II

[1] "God Moves in a Mysterious Way," included in most hymnals.

[2] Ruth Bell Graham, *Legacy of a Pack Rat* (Nashville: Oliver Nelson, 1989), pp. 37-39.

[3] *Guideposts*, January 1991, pp. 24-28.

[4] H. G. Bosch, *Our Daily Bread*, March 6, 1991.

[5] *Memorials of a Quiet Life: A Memoir of Richard F. Varder* (Grand Rapids: Gospel Folio Press, 1934), p. 119.

[6] *Assembly Annals*, August 1946.

[7] Mark Wheeler, "Secure in the Storm," *Kindred Spirit Magazine*, Summer 1986, pp. 8-10.

[8] H. G. Bosch, *Our Daily Bread*, April 12, 1986.

[9] "Two O'Clock at Entebbe," *Uplook Magazine*, February 1991, pp. 12-14.

[10] Percy O. Ruoff, *W. E. Vine: His Life and Ministry* (London: Oliphants Ltd., 1951), pp. 18-19.

[11] Source: Olive Fleming Liefeld, *Unfolding Destinies* (Grand Rapids: Zondervan Publishing House), 1990, pp. 235-37.

[12] G. C. Willis, *I Was Among the Captives* (Hong Kong: Bible Light Publishers, n.d.), pp. 84-89.

[13] From *Our Daily Bread*, reading for Saturday, September 7, 1991.

[14] From *Our Daily Bread*, Tuesday, April 21, 1992.

[15] Dr. J. Allen Blair, *Profile of a Christian* (Westchester, IL: Good News Publishers, n.d.), pp. 30-31.

[16] Tony Lawman, *From the Hands of the Wicked* (London: Robert Hale Ltd., 1960), pp. 63-64.

[17] Ibid., p. 42.

[18] Ibid., p. 44.

[19] Ibid., pp. 44-45.

[20] Charles Haddon Spurgeon, *Treasury of the Old Testament* (Grand Rapids: Baker Book House, 1981), IV:212.

PART III

[1] J. H. Jowett, *The Best of John H. Jowett* (Grand Rapids: Baker Book House, 1981), p. 14.

[2] Sikhism is a religion in India that seeks to merge Muslim and Hindu teaching into one religion.

[3] Archie Naismith, *1200 More Notes, Quotes, and Anecdotes* (London: Pickering & Inglis Ltd., 1975), p. 27.

[4] *Our Daily Bread*, April 19, 1989.

[5] F. W. Boreham, *A Bunch of Everlastings* (London: The Epworth Press, 1926), p. 60.

[6] C. S. Lewis, *Surprised by Joy* (New York: Harcourt Brace Jovanovich, Publishers, 1956), p. 211.

[7] Calling the Lord "The Hound of Heaven" is from the famous poem of the same name by Francis Thompson.

[8] Lewis, *Surprised by Joy*, p. 226.

[9] Ibid., p. 228.

[10] Ibid., pp. 228-29.

[11] Ibid., p. 229.

[12] *Spurgeon, the Early Years* (London: The Banner of Truth Trust, 1967), p. 267.

[13] Charles Haddon Spurgeon, *Treasury of the Bible* (Grand Rapids: Baker Book House, 1981), 8:370.

[14] Adapted from "How to Rise Above Discouragement," *Discipleship Journal*, July 1982.

[15] Adapted from UNSHACKLED tape #544, Pacific Garden Mission, Chicago.

[16] As recounted by David Long, formerly of Angola.

[17] As recounted by Dorothy Harris, of Tehuacan, Mexico

[18] As recounted by Dr. Betty Brooks, formerly of Lusaka, Zambia.